Alarms And Discursions

By

G. K. Chesterton

Contents

Introductory: On Gargoyles 1
The Surrender of a Cockney 4
The Nightmare 7
The Telegraph Poles 10
A Drama of Dolls 13
The Man and His Newspaper 15
The Appetite of Earth 18
Simmons and the Social Tie 20
Cheese 23
The Red Town 25
   The Furrows 28
   The Philosophy of Sight-seeing 30
   A Criminal Head 33
   The Wrath of the Roses 36
   The Gold of Glastonbury 38
   The Futurists 40
   Dukes 43
   The Glory of Grey 46
   The Anarchist 49
   How I found the Superman 52
   The New House 55
   The Wings of Stone 57
   The Three Kinds of Men 59
   The Steward of the Chiltern Hundreds 62
   The Field of Blood 64
   The Strangeness of Luxury 66
   The Triumph of the Donkey 69
   The Wheel 72
   Five Hundred and Fifty-five 74
   Ethandune 76
   The Flat Freak 79
   The Garden of the Sea 82
   The Sentimentalist 84
   The White Horses 87
   The Long Bow 90
   The Modern Scrooge 93
   The High Plains 97
   The Chorus 99
   A Romance of the Marshes 102

Introductory: On Gargoyles

Alone at some distance from the wasting walls of a disused abbey I found half sunken in the grass the grey and goggle-eyed visage of one of those graven monsters that made the ornamental water-spouts in the cathedrals of the Middle Ages. It lay there, scoured by ancient rains or striped by recent fungus, but still looking like the head of some huge dragon slain by a primeval hero. And as I looked at it, I thought of the meaning of the grotesque, and passed into some symbolic reverie of the three great stages of art.

I

Once upon a time there lived upon an island a merry and innocent people, mostly shepherds and tillers of the earth. They were republicans, like all primitive and simple souls; they talked over their affairs under a tree, and the nearest approach they had to a personal ruler was a sort of priest or white witch who said their prayers for them. They worshipped the sun, not idolatrously, but as the golden crown of the god whom all such infants see almost as plainly as the sun.

Now this priest was told by his people to build a great tower, pointing to the sky in salutation of the Sun-god; and he pondered long and heavily before he picked his materials. For he was resolved to use nothing that was not almost as clear and exquisite as sunshine itself; he would use nothing that was not washed as white as the rain can wash the heavens, nothing that did not sparkle as spotlessly as that crown of God. He would have nothing grotesque or obscure; he would not have even anything emphatic or even anything mysterious. He would have all the arches as light as laughter and as candid as logic. He built the temple in three concentric courts, which were cooler and more exquisite in substance each than the other. For the outer wall was a hedge of white lilies, ranked so thick that a green stalk was hardly to be seen; and the wall within that was of crystal, which smashed the sun into a million stars. And the wall within that, which was the tower itself, was a tower of pure water, forced up in an everlasting fountain; and upon the very tip and crest of that foaming spire was one big and blazing diamond, which the water tossed up eternally and caught again as a child catches a ball.

"Now," said the priest, "I have made a tower which is a little worthy of the sun."

II

But about this time the island was caught in a swarm of pirates; and the shepherds had to turn themselves into rude warriors and seamen; and at first they were utterly broken down in blood and shame; and the pirates might have taken the jewel flung up for ever from their sacred fount. And then, after years of horror and humiliation, they gained a little and began to conquer because they did not mind defeat. And the pride of the pirates went sick within them after a few unexpected foils; and at last the invasion rolled back into the empty seas and the island was delivered. And for some reason after this men began to talk quite differently about the temple and the sun. Some, indeed, said, "You must not touch the temple; it is classical; it is perfect, since it admits no imperfections." But the others answered, "In that it differs from the sun, that shines on the evil and the good and on mud and monsters everywhere. The temple is of the noon; it is made of white marble clouds and sapphire sky. But the sun is not always of the noon. The sun dies daily, every night he is crucified in blood and fire." Now the priest had taught and fought through all the war, and his hair had grown white, but his eyes had grown young. And he said, "I was wrong and they are right. The sun, the symbol of our father, gives life to all those earthly things that are full of ugliness and energy. All the exaggerations are right, if they exaggerate the right thing. Let us point to heaven with tusks and horns and fins and trunks and tails so long as they all point to heaven. The ugly animals praise God as much as the beautiful. The frog's eyes stand out of his head because he is staring at heaven. The giraffe's neck is long because he is stretching towards heaven. The donkey has ears to hear—let him hear."

And under the new inspiration they planned a gorgeous cathedral in the Gothic manner, with all the animals of the earth crawling over it, and all the possible ugly things making up one common beauty, because they all appealed to the god. The columns of the temple were carved like the necks of giraffes; the dome was like an ugly tortoise; and the highest pinnacle was a monkey standing on his head with his tail pointing at the sun. And yet the whole was beautiful, because it was lifted up in one living and religious gesture as a man lifts his hands in prayer.

III

But this great plan was never properly completed. The people had brought up on great wagons the heavy tortoise roof and the huge necks of stone, and all the thousand and one oddities that made up that unity, the owls and the efts and the crocodiles and the kangaroos, which hideous by themselves might have been magnificent if reared in one definite proportion and dedicated to the sun. For this was Gothic, this was romantic, this was Christian art; this was the whole advance of Shakespeare upon Sophocles. And that symbol which was to crown it all, the ape upside down, was really Christian; for man is the ape upside down.

But the rich, who had grown riotous in the long peace, obstructed the thing, and in some squabble a stone struck the priest on the head and he lost his memory. He saw piled in front of him frogs and elephants, monkeys and giraffes, toadstools and sharks, all the ugly things of the universe which he had collected to do honour to God. But he forgot why he had collected them. He could not remember the design or the object. He piled them all wildly into one heap fifty feet high; and when he had done it all the rich and influential went into a passion of applause and cried, "This is real art! This is Realism! This is things as they really are!"

Alarms and Discursions

That, I fancy, is the only true origin of Realism. Realism is simply Romanticism that has lost its reason. This is so not merely in the sense of insanity but of suicide. It has lost its reason; that is its reason for existing. The old Greeks summoned godlike things to worship their god. The medieval Christians summoned all things to worship theirs, dwarfs and pelicans, monkeys and madmen. The modern realists summon all these million creatures to worship their god; and then have no god for them to worship. Paganism was in art a pure beauty; that was the dawn. Christianity was a beauty created by controlling a million monsters of ugliness; and that in my belief was the zenith and the noon. Modern art and science practically mean having the million monsters and being unable to control them; and I will venture to call that the disruption and the decay. The finest lengths of the Elgin marbles consist splendid houses going to the temple of a virgin. Christianity, with its gargoyles and grotesques, really amounted to saying this: that a donkey could go before all the horses of the world when it was really going to the temple. Romance means a holy donkey going to the temple. Realism means a lost donkey going nowhere.

The fragments of futile journalism or fleeting impression which are here collected are very like the wrecks and riven blocks that were piled in a heap round my imaginary priest of the sun. They are very like that grey and gaping head of stone that I found overgrown with the grass. Yet I will venture to make even of these trivial fragments the high boast that I am a medievalist and not a modern. That is, I really have a notion of why I have collected all the nonsensical things there are. I have not the patience nor perhaps the constructive intelligence to state the connecting link between all these chaotic papers. But it could be stated. This row of shapeless and ungainly monsters which I now set before the reader does not consist of separate idols cut out capriciously in lonely valleys or various islands. These monsters are meant for the gargoyles of a definite cathedral. I have to carve the gargoyles, because I can carve nothing else; I leave to others the angels and the arches and the spires. But I am very sure of the style of the architecture, and of the consecration of the church.

G. K. Chesterton

The Surrender of a Cockney

Evert man, though he were born in the very belfry of Bow and spent his infancy climbing among chimneys, has waiting for him somewhere a country house which he has never seen; but which was built for him in the very shape of his soul. It stands patiently waiting to be found, knee-deep in orchards of Kent or mirrored in pools of Lincoln; and when the man sees it he remembers it, though he has never seen it before. Even I have been forced to confess this at last, who am a Cockney, if ever there was one, a Cockney not only on principle, but with savage pride. I have always maintained, quite seriously, that the Lord is not in the wind or thunder of the waste, but if anywhere in the still small voice of Fleet Street. I sincerely maintain that Nature-worship is more morally dangerous than the most vulgar man-worship of the cities; since it can easily be perverted into the worship of an impersonal mystery, carelessness, or cruelty. Thoreau would have been a jollier fellow if he had devoted himself to a greengrocer instead of to greens. Swinburne would have been a better moralist if he had worshipped a fishmonger instead of worshipping the sea. I prefer the philosophy of bricks and mortar to the philosophy of turnips. To call a man a turnip may be playful, but is seldom respectful. But when we wish to pay emphatic honour to a man, to praise the firmness of his nature, the squareness of his conduct, the strong humility with which he is interlocked with his equals in silent mutual support, then we invoke the nobler Cockney metaphor, and call him a brick.

But, despite all these theories, I have surrendered; I have struck my colours at sight; at a mere glimpse through the opening of a hedge. I shall come down to living in the country, like any common Socialist or Simple Lifer. I shall end my days in a village, in the character of the Village Idiot, and be a spectacle and a judgment to mankind. I have already learnt the rustic manner of leaning upon a gate; and I was thus gymnastically occupied at the moment when my eye caught the house that was made for me. It stood well back from the road, and was built of a good yellow brick; it was narrow for its height, like the tower of some Border robber; and over the front door was carved in large letters, "1908." That last burst of sincerity, that superb scorn of antiquarian sentiment, overwhelmed me finally. I closed my eyes in a kind of ecstasy. My friend (who was helping me to lean on the gate) asked me with some curiosity what I was doing.

"My dear fellow," I said, with emotion, "I am bidding farewell to forty-three hansom cabmen."

"Well," he said, "I suppose they would think this county rather outside the radius."

"Oh, my friend," I cried brokenly, "how beautiful London is! Why do they only write poetry about the country? I could turn every lyric cry into Cockney.

"'My heart leaps up when I behold A sky-sign in the sky,'

"as I observed in a volume which is too little read, founded on the older English poets. You never saw my 'Golden Treasury Regilded; or, The Classics Made Cockney'—it contained some fine lines.

"'O Wild West End, thou breath of London's being,'

"or the reminiscence of Keats, beginning

"'City of smuts and mellow fogfulness.';

"I have written many such lines on the beauty of London; yet I never realized that London was really beautiful till now. Do you ask me why? It is because I have left it for ever."

"If you will take my advice," said my friend, "you will humbly endeavour not to be a fool. What is the sense of this mad modern notion that every literary man must live in the country, with the pigs and the donkeys and the squires? Chaucer and Spenser and Milton and Dryden lived in London; Shakespeare and Dr. Johnson came to London because they had had quite enough of the country. And as for trumpery topical journalists like you, why, they would cut their throats in the country. You have confessed it yourself in your own last words. You hunger and thirst after the streets; you think London the finest place on the planet. And if by some miracle a Bayswater omnibus could come down this green country lane you would utter a yell of joy."

Then a light burst upon my brain, and I turned upon him with terrible sternness.

"Why, miserable aesthete," I said in a voice of thunder, "that is the true country spirit! That is how the real rustic feels. The real rustic does utter a yell of joy at the sight of a Bayswater omnibus. The real rustic does think London the finest place on the planet. In the few moments that I have stood by this stile, I have grown rooted here like an ancient tree; I have been here for ages. Petulant Suburban, I am the real rustic. I believe that the streets of London are paved with gold; and I mean to see it before I die."

The evening breeze freshened among the little tossing trees of that lane, and the purple evening clouds piled up and darkened behind my Country Seat, the house that belonged to me, making, by contrast, its yellow bricks gleam like gold. At last my friend said: "To cut it short, then, you mean that you will live in the country because you won't like it. What on earth will you do here; dig up the garden?"

"Dig!" I answered, in honourable scorn. "Dig! Do work at my Country Seat; no, thank you. When I find a Country Seat, I sit in it. And for your other objection, you are quite wrong. I do not dislike the country, but I like the town more. Therefore the art of happiness certainly suggests that I should live in the country and think about the town. Modern nature-worship is all upside down. Trees and fields ought to be the ordinary

G. K. Chesterton

things; terraces and temples ought to be extraordinary. I am on the side of the man who lives in the country and wants to go to London. I abominate and abjure the man who lives in London and wants to go to the country; I do it with all the more heartiness because I am that sort of man myself. We must learn to love London again, as rustics love it. Therefore (I quote again from the great Cockney version of The Golden Treasury)—

" 'Therefore, ye gas-pipes, ye asbestos? stoves,
Forbode not any severing of our loves.
I have relinquished but your earthly sight,
To hold you dear in a more distant way.
I'll love the 'buses lumbering through the wet,
Even more than when I lightly tripped as they.
The grimy colour of the London clay Is lovely yet,'

"because I have found the house where I was really born; the tall and quiet house from which I can see London afar off, as the miracle of man that it is."

The Nightmare

A sunset of copper and gold had just broken down and gone to pieces in the west, and grey colours were crawling over everything in earth and heaven; also a wind was growing, a wind that laid a cold finger upon flesh and spirit. The bushes at the back of my garden began to whisper like conspirators; and then to wave like wild hands in signal. I was trying to read by the last light that died on the lawn a long poem of the decadent period, a poem about the old gods of Babylon and Egypt, about their blazing and obscene temples, their cruel and colossal faces.

"Or didst thou love the God of Flies who plagued the Hebrews and was splashed With wine unto the waist, or Pasht who had green beryls for her eyes?"

I read this poem because I had to review it for the Daily News; still it was genuine poetry of its kind. It really gave out an atmosphere, a fragrant and suffocating smoke that seemed really to come from the Bondage of Egypt or the Burden of Tyre There is not much in common (thank God) between my garden with the grey-green English sky-line beyond it, and these mad visions of painted palaces huge, headless idols and monstrous solitudes of red or golden sand. Nevertheless (as I confessed to myself) I can fancy in such a stormy twilight some such smell of death and fear. The ruined sunset really looks like one of their ruined temples: a shattered heap of gold and green marble. A black flapping thing detaches itself from one of the sombre trees and flutters to another. I know not if it is owl or flittermouse; I could fancy it was a black cherub, an infernal cherub of darkness, not with the wings of a bird and the head of a baby, but with the head of a goblin and the wings of a bat. I think, if there were light enough, I could sit here and write some very creditable creepy tale, about how I went up the crooked road beyond the church and met Something—say a dog, a dog with one eye. Then I should meet a horse, perhaps, a horse without a rider, the horse also would have one eye. Then the inhuman silence would be broken; I should meet a man (need I say, a one-eyed man?) who would ask me the way to my own house. Or perhaps tell me that it was burnt to the ground. I could tell a very cosy little tale along some such lines. Or I might dream of climbing for ever the tall dark trees above me. They are so tall that I feel as if I should find at their tops the nests of the angels; but in this mood they would be dark and dreadful angels; angels of death.

Only, you see, this mood is all bosh. I do not believe in it in the least. That one-eyed universe, with its one-eyed men and beasts, was only created with one universal wink. At the top of the tragic trees I should not find the Angel's Nest. I should only find the Mare's Nest; the dreamy and divine nest is not there. In the Mare's Nest I shall discover that dim, enormous opalescent egg from which is hatched the Nightmare. For there is nothing so delightful as a nightmare—when you know it is a nightmare.

That is the essential. That is the stern condition laid upon all artists touching this luxury of fear. The terror must be fundamentally frivolous. Sanity may play with insanity; but insanity must not be allowed to play with sanity. Let such poets as the one I was reading in the garden, by all means, be free to imagine what outrageous deities and violent landscapes they like. By all means let them wander freely amid their opium pinnacles and perspectives. But these huge gods, these high cities, are toys; they must never for an instant be allowed to be anything else. Man, a gigantic child, must play with Babylon and Nineveh, with Isis and with Ashtaroth. By all means let him dream of the Bondage of Egypt, so long as he is free from it. By all means let him take up the Burden of Tyre, so long as he can take it lightly. But the old gods must be his dolls, not his idols. His central sanctities, his true possessions, should be Christian and simple. And just as a child would cherish most a wooden horse or a sword that is a mere cross of wood, so man, the great child, must cherish most the old plain things of poetry and piety; that horse of wood that was the epic end of Ilium, or that cross of wood that redeemed and conquered the world.

In one of Stevenson's letters there is a characteristically humorous remark about the appalling impression produced on him in childhood by the beasts with many eyes in the Book of Revelations: "If that was heaven, what in the name of Davy Jones was hell like?" Now in sober truth there is a magnificent idea in these monsters of the Apocalypse. It is, I suppose, the idea that beings really more beautiful or more universal than we are might appear to us frightful and even confused. Especially they might seem to have senses at once more multiplex and more staring; an idea very imaginatively seized in the multitude of eyes. I like those monsters beneath the throne very much. But I like them beneath the throne. It is when one of them goes wandering in deserts and finds a throne for himself that evil faiths begin, and there is (literally) the devil to pay—to pay in dancing girls or human sacrifice. As long as those misshapen elemental powers are around the throne, remember that the thing that they worship is the likeness of the appearance of a man.

That is, I fancy, the true doctrine on the subject of Tales of Terror and such things, which unless a man of letters do well and truly believe, without doubt he will end by blowing his brains out or by writing badly. Man, the central pillar of the world must be upright and straight; around him all the trees and beasts and elements and devils may crook and curl like smoke if they choose. All really imaginative literature is only the contrast between the weird curves of Nature and the straightness of the soul. Man may behold what ugliness he likes if he is sure that he will not worship it; but there are some so weak that they will worship a thing only because it is ugly. These must be chained to the beautiful. It is not always wrong even to go, like Dante, to the brink of the lowest promontory and look down at hell. It is when you look up at hell that a serious miscalculation has probably been made.

Alarms and Discursions

Therefore I see no wrong in riding with the Nightmare to-night; she whinnies to me from the rocking tree-tops and the roaring wind; I will catch her and ride her through the awful air. Woods and weeds are alike tugging at the roots in the rising tempest, as if all wished to fly with us over the moon, like that wild amorous cow whose child was the Moon-Calf. We will rise to that mad infinite where there is neither up nor down, the high topsy-turveydom of the heavens. I will answer the call of chaos and old night. I will ride on the Nightmare; but she shall not ride on me.

G. K. Chesterton

The Telegraph Poles

My friend and I were walking in one of those wastes of pine-wood which make inland seas of solitude in every part of Western Europe; which have the true terror of a desert, since they are uniform, and so one may lose one's way in them. Stiff, straight, and similar, stood up all around us the pines of the wood, like the pikes of a silent mutiny. There is a truth in talking of the variety of Nature; but I think that Nature often shows her chief strangeness in her sameness. There is a weird rhythm in this very repetition; it is as if the earth were resolved to repeat a single shape until the shape shall turn terrible.

Have you ever tried the experiment of saying some plain word, such as "dog," thirty times? By the thirtieth time it has become a word like "snark" or "pobble." It does not become tame, it becomes wild, by repetition. In the end a dog walks about as startling and undecipherable as Leviathan or Croquemitaine.

It may be that this explains the repetitions in Nature, it may be for this reason that there are so many million leaves and pebbles. Perhaps they are not repeated so that they may grow familiar. Perhaps they are repeated only in the hope that they may at last grow unfamiliar. Perhaps a man is not startled at the first cat he sees, but jumps into the air with surprise at the seventy-ninth cat. Perhaps he has to pass through thousands of pine trees before he finds the one that is really a pine tree. However this may be, there is something singularly thrilling, even something urgent and intolerant, about the endless forest repetitions; there is the hint of something like madness in that musical monotony of the pines.

I said something like this to my friend; and he answered with sardonic truth, "Ah, you wait till we come to a telegraph post."

My friend was right, as he occasionally is in our discussions, especially upon points of fact. We had crossed the pine forest by one of its paths which happened to follow the wires of the provincial telegraphy; and though the poles occurred at long intervals they made a difference when they came. The instant we came to the straight pole we could see that the pines were not really straight. It was like a hundred straight lines drawn with schoolboy pencils all brought to judgment suddenly by one straight line drawn with a ruler. All the amateur lines seemed to reel to right and left. A moment before I could have sworn they stood as straight as lances; now I could see them curve and waver everywhere, like scimitars and yataghans. Compared with the telegraph post the pines were crooked—and alive. That lonely vertical rod at once deformed and enfranchised the forest. It tangled it all together and yet made it free, like any grotesque undergrowth of oak or holly.

"Yes," said my gloomy friend, answering my thoughts. "You don't know what a wicked shameful thing straightness is if you think these trees are straight. You never will know till your precious intellectual civilization builds a forty-mile forest of telegraph poles."

Alarms and Discursions

We had started walking from our temporary home later in the day than we intended; and the long afternoon was already lengthening itself out into a yellow evening when we came out of the forest on to the hills above a strange town or village, of which the lights had already begun to glitter in the darkening valley. The change had already happened which is the test and definition of evening. I mean that while the sky seemed still as bright, the earth was growing blacker against it, especially at the edges, the hills and the pine-tops. This brought out yet more clearly the owlish secrecy of pine-woods; and my friend cast a regretful glance at them as he came out under the sky. Then he turned to the view in front; and, as it happened, one of the telegraph posts stood up in front of him in the last sunlight. It was no longer crossed and softened by the more delicate lines of pine wood; it stood up ugly, arbitrary, and angular as any crude figure in geometry. My friend stopped, pointing his stick at it, and all his anarchic philosophy rushed to his lips.

"Demon," he said to me briefly, "behold your work. That palace of proud trees behind us is what the world was before you civilized men, Christians or democrats or the rest, came to make it dull with your dreary rules of morals and equality. In the silent fight of that forest, tree fights speechless against tree, branch against branch. And the upshot of that dumb battle is inequality—and beauty. Now lift up your eyes and look at equality and ugliness. See how regularly the white buttons are arranged on that black stick, and defend your dogmas if you dare."

"Is that telegraph post so much a symbol of democracy?" I asked. "I fancy that while three men have made the telegraph to get dividends, about a thousand men have preserved the forest to cut wood. But if the telegraph pole is hideous (as I admit) it is not due to doctrine but rather to commercial anarchy. If any one had a doctrine about a telegraph pole it might be carved in ivory and decked with gold. Modern things are ugly, because modern men are careless, not because they are careful."

"No," answered my friend with his eye on the end of a splendid and sprawling sunset, "there is something intrinsically deadening about the very idea of a doctrine. A straight line is always ugly. Beauty is always crooked. These rigid posts at regular intervals are ugly because they are carrying across the world the real message of democracy."

"At this moment," I answered, "they are probably carrying across the world the message, 'Buy Bulgarian Rails.' They are probably the prompt communication between some two of the wealthiest and wickedest of His children with whom God has ever had patience. No; these telegraph poles are ugly and detestable, they are inhuman and indecent. But their baseness lies in their privacy, not in their publicity. That black stick with white buttons is not the creation of the soul of a multitude. It is the mad creation of the souls of two millionaires."

"At least you have to explain," answered my friend gravely, "how it is that the hard democratic doctrine and the hard telegraphic outline have appeared together; you have... But bless my soul, we must be getting home. I had no idea it was so late. Let me see, I think this is our way through the wood. Come, let us both curse the telegraph post for entirely different reasons and get home before it is dark."

We did not get home before it was dark. For one reason or another we had underestimated the swiftness of twilight and the suddenness of night, especially in the threading of thick woods. When my friend, after the first five minutes' march, had fallen over a log, and I, ten minutes after, had stuck nearly to the knees in mire, we began to have some suspicion of our direction. At last my friend said, in a low, husky voice:

"I'm afraid we're on the wrong path. It's pitch dark."

"I thought we went the right way," I said, tentatively.

"Well," he said; and then, after a long pause, "I can't see any telegraph poles. I've been looking for them."

"So have I," I said. "They're so straight."

We groped away for about two hours of darkness in the thick of the fringe of trees which seemed to dance round us in derision. Here and there, however, it was possible to trace the outline of something just too erect and rigid to be a pine tree. By these we finally felt our way home, arriving in a cold green twilight before dawn.

A Drama of Dolls

In a small grey town of stone in one of the great Yorkshire dales, which is full of history, I entered a hall and saw an old puppet-play exactly as our fathers saw it five hundred years ago. It was admirably translated from the old German, and was the original tale of Faust. The dolls were at once comic and convincing; but if you cannot at once laugh at a thing and believe in it, you have no business in the Middle Ages. Or in the world, for that matter.

The puppet-play in question belongs, I believe, to the fifteenth century; and indeed the whole legend of Dr. Faustus has the colour of that grotesque but somewhat gloomy time. It is very unfortunate that we so often know a thing that is past only by its tail end. We remember yesterday only by its sunsets. There are many instances. One is Napoleon. We always think of him as a fat old despot, ruling Europe with a ruthless military machine. But that, as Lord Rosebery would say, was only "The Last Phase"; or at least the last but one. During the strongest and most startling part of his career, the time that made him immortal, Napoleon was a sort of boy, and not a bad sort of boy either, bullet-headed and ambitious, but honestly in love with a woman, and honestly enthusiastic for a cause, the cause of French justice and equality.

Another instance is the Middle Ages, which we also remember only by the odour of their ultimate decay. We think of the life of the Middle Ages as a dance of death, full of devils and deadly sins, lepers and burning heretics. But this was not the life of the Middle Ages, but the death of the Middle Ages. It is the spirit of Louis XI and Richard III, not of Louis IX and Edward I.

This grim but not unwholesome fable of Dr. Faustus, with its rebuke to the mere arrogance of learning, is sound and stringent enough; but it is not a fair sample of the mediaeval soul at its happiest and sanest. The heart of the true Middle Ages might be found far better, for instance, in the noble tale of Tannhauser, in which the dead staff broke into leaf and flower to rebuke the pontiff who had declared even one human being beyond the strength of sorrow and pardon.

But there were in the play two great human ideas which the mediaeval mind never lost its grip on, through the heaviest nightmares of its dissolution. They were the two great jokes of mediaevalism, as they are the two eternal jokes of mankind. Wherever those two jokes exist there is a little health and hope; wherever they are absent, pride and insanity are present. The first is the idea that the poor man ought to get the better of the rich man. The other is the idea that the husband is afraid of the wife.

I have heard that there is a place under the knee which, when struck, should produce a sort of jump; and that if you do not jump, you are mad. I am sure that there are some such places in the soul. When the human spirit does not jump with joy at either of those two old jokes, the human spirit must be struck with incurable paralysis. There is hope for people who have gone down into the hells of greed and economic oppression (at least, I hope there is, for we are such a people ourselves), but there is no hope for a people that does not exult in the abstract idea of the peasant scoring off the prince. There is hope for the idle and the adulterous, for the men that desert their wives and the men that beat their wives. But there is no hope for men who do not boast that their wives bully them.

The first idea, the idea about the man at the bottom coming out on top, is expressed in this puppet-play in the person of Dr. Faustus' servant, Caspar. Sentimental old Tones, regretting the feudal times, sometimes complain that in these days Jack is as good as his master. But most of the actual tales of the feudal times turn on the idea that Jack is much better than his master, and certainly it is so in the case of Caspar and Faust. The play ends with the damnation of the learned and illustrious doctor, followed by a cheerful and animated dance by Caspar, who has been made watchman of the city.

But there was a much keener stroke of mediaeval irony earlier in the play. The learned doctor has been ransacking all the libraries of the earth to find a certain rare formula, now almost unknown, by which he can control the infernal deities. At last he procures the one precious volume, opens it at the proper page, and leaves it on the table while he seeks some other part of his magic equipment. The servant comes in, reads off the formula, and immediately becomes an emperor of the elemental spirits. He gives them a horrible time. He summons and dismisses them alternately with the rapidity of a piston-rod working at high speed; he keeps them flying between the doctor's house and their own more unmentionable residences till they faint with rage and fatigue. There is all the best of the Middle Ages in that; the idea of the great levellers, luck and laughter; the idea of a sense of humour defying and dominating hell.

One of the best points in the play as performed in this Yorkshire town was that the servant Caspar was made to talk Yorkshire, instead of the German rustic dialect which he talked in the original. That also smacks of the good air of that epoch. In those old pictures and poems they always made things living by making them local. Thus, queerly enough, the one touch that was not in the old mediaeval version was the most mediaeval touch of all.

That other ancient and Christian jest, that a wife is a holy terror, occurs in the last scene, where the doctor (who wears a fur coat throughout, to make him seem more offensively rich and refined) is attempting to escape from the avenging demons, and meets his old servant in the street. The servant obligingly points out a house with a blue door, and strongly recommends Dr. Faustus to take refuge in it. "My old woman lives there," he says, "and the devils are more afraid of her than you are of them." Faustus does not take this advice, but goes on meditating and reflecting (which had been his mistake all along) until the clock strikes twelve, and dreadful voices talk Latin in heaven. So Faustus, in his fur coat, is carried away by little black imps; and serve him right for being an Intellectual.

The Man and His Newspaper

At a little station, which I decline to specify, somewhere between Oxford and Guildford, I missed a connection or miscalculated a route in such manner that I was left stranded for rather more than an hour. I adore waiting at railway stations, but this was not a very sumptuous specimen. There was nothing on the platform except a chocolate automatic machine, which eagerly absorbed pennies but produced no corresponding chocolate, and a small paper-stall with a few remaining copies of a cheap imperial organ which we will call the Daily Wire. It does not matter which imperial organ it was, as they all say the same thing.

Though I knew it quite well already, I read it with gravity as I strolled out of the station and up the country road. It opened with the striking phrase that the Radicals were setting class against class. It went on to remark that nothing had contributed more to make our Empire happy and enviable, to create that obvious list of glories which you can supply for yourself, the prosperity of all classes in our great cities, our populous and growing villages, the success of our rule in Ireland, etc., etc., than the sound Anglo-Saxon readiness of all classes in the State "to work heartily hand-in-hand." It was this alone, the paper assured me, that had saved us from the horrors of the French Revolution. "It is easy for the Radicals," it went on very solemnly, "to make jokes about the dukes. Very few of these revolutionary gentlemen have given to the poor one half of the earnest thought, tireless unselfishness, and truly Christian patience that are given to them by the great landlords of this country. We are very sure that the English people, with their sturdy common sense, will prefer to be in the hands of English gentlemen rather than in the miry claws of Socialistic buccaneers."

Just when I had reached this point I nearly ran into a man. Despite the populousness and growth of our villages, he appeared to be the only man for miles, but the road up which I had wandered turned and narrowed with equal abruptness, and I nearly knocked him off the gate on which he was leaning. I pulled up to apologize, and since he seemed ready for society, and even pathetically pleased with it, I tossed the Daily Wire over a hedge and fell into speech with him. He wore a wreck of respectable clothes, and his face had that plebeian refinement which one sees in small tailors and watchmakers, in poor men of sedentary trades. Behind him a twisted group of winter trees stood up as gaunt and tattered as himself, but I do not think that the tragedy that he symbolized was a mere fancy from the spectral wood. There was a fixed look in his face which told that he was one of those who in keeping body and soul together have difficulties not only with the body, but also with the soul.

He was a Cockney by birth, and retained the touching accent of those streets from which I am an exile; but he had lived nearly all his life in this countryside; and he began to tell me the affairs of it in that formless, tail-foremost way in which the poor gossip about their great neighbours.

G. K. Chesterton

Names kept coming and going in the narrative like charms or spells, unaccompanied by any biographical explanation. In particular the name of somebody called Sir Joseph multiplied itself with the omnipresence of a deity. I took Sir Joseph to be the principal landowner of the district; and as the confused picture unfolded itself, I began to form a definite and by no means pleasing picture of Sir Joseph. He was spoken of in a strange way, frigid and yet familiar, as a child might speak of a stepmother or an unavoidable nurse; something intimate, but by no means tender; something that was waiting for you by your own bed and board; that told you to do this and forbade you to do that, with a caprice that was cold and yet somehow personal. It did not appear that Sir Joseph was popular, but he was "a household word." He was not so much a public man as a sort of private god or omnipotence. The particular man to whom I spoke said he had "been in trouble," and that Sir Joseph had been "pretty hard on him."

And under that grey and silver cloudland, with a background of those frost-bitten and wind-tortured trees, the little Londoner told me a tale which, true or false, was as heartrending as Romeo and Juliet.

He had slowly built up in the village a small business as a photographer, and he was engaged to a girl at one of the lodges, whom he loved with passion. "I'm the sort that 'ad better marry," he said; and for all his frail figure I knew what he meant. But Sir Joseph, and especially Sir Joseph's wife, did not want a photographer in the village; it made the girls vain, or perhaps they disliked this particular photographer. He worked and worked until he had just enough to marry on honestly; and almost on the eve of his wedding the lease expired, and Sir Joseph appeared in all his glory. He refused to renew the lease; and the man went wildly elsewhere. But Sir Joseph was ubiquitous; and the whole of that place was barred against him. In all that country he could not find a shed to which to bring home his bride. The man appealed and explained; but he was disliked as a demagogue, as well as a photographer. Then it was as if a black cloud came across the winter sky; for I knew what was coming. I forget even in what words he told of Nature maddened and set free. But I still see, as in a photograph, the grey muscles of the winter trees standing out like tight ropes, as if all Nature were on the rack.

"She 'ad to go away," he said.

"Wouldn't her parents," I began, and hesitated on the word "forgive."

"Oh, her people forgave her," he said. "But Her Ladyship..."

"Her Ladyship made the sun and moon and stars," I said, impatiently. "So of course she can come between a mother and the child of her body."

"Well, it does seem a bit 'ard..." he began with a break in his voice.

"But, good Lord, man," I cried, "it isn't a matter of hardness! It's a matter of impious and indecent wickedness. If your Sir Joseph knew the passions he was playing with, he did you a wrong for which in many Christian countries he would have a knife in him."

The man continued to look across the frozen fields with a frown. He certainly told his tale with real resentment, whether it was true or false, or only exaggerated. He was certainly sullen and injured; but he did not seem to think of any avenue of escape. At last he said:

"Well, it's a bad world; let's 'ope there's a better one."

"Amen," I said. "But when I think of Sir Joseph, I understand how men have hoped there was a worse one."

Then we were silent for a long time and felt the cold of the day crawling up, and at last I said, abruptly:

"The other day at a Budget meeting, I heard."

He took his elbows off the stile and seemed to change from head to foot like a man coming out of sleep with a yawn. He said in a totally new voice, louder but much more careless, "Ah yes, sir,... this 'ere Budget... the Radicals are doing a lot of 'arm."

I listened intently, and he went on. He said with a sort of careful precision, "Settin' class against class; that's what I call it. Why, what's made our Empire except the readiness of all classes to work 'eartily 'and-in-'and."

He walked a little up and down the lane and stamped with the cold. Then he said, "What I say is, what else kept us from the 'errors of the French Revolution?"

My memory is good, and I waited in tense eagerness for the phrase that came next. "They may laugh at Dukes; I'd like to see them 'alf as kind and Christian and patient as lots of the landlords are. Let me tell you, sir," he said, facing round at me with the final air of one launching a paradox. "The English people 'ave some common sense, and they'd rather be in the 'ands of gentlemen than in the claws of a lot of Socialist thieves."

I had an indescribable sense that I ought to applaud, as if I were a public meeting. The insane separation in the man's soul between his experience and his ready-made theory was but a type of what covers a quarter of England. As he turned away, I saw the Daily Wire sticking out of his shabby pocket. He bade me farewell in quite a blaze of catchwords, and went stumping up the road. I saw his figure grow smaller and smaller in the great green landscape; even as the Free Man has grown smaller and smaller in the English countryside.

G. K. Chesterton

The Appetite of Earth

I was walking the other day in a kitchen garden, which I find has somehow got attached to my premises, and I was wondering why I liked it. After a prolonged spiritual self-analysis I came to the conclusion that I like a kitchen garden because it contains things to eat. I do not mean that a kitchen garden is ugly; a kitchen garden is often very beautiful. The mixture of green and purple on some monstrous cabbage is much subtler and grander than the mere freakish and theatrical splashing of yellow and violet on a pansy. Few of the flowers merely meant for ornament are so ethereal as a potato. A kitchen garden is as beautiful as an orchard; but why is it that the word "orchard" sounds as beautiful as the word "flower-garden," and yet also sounds more satisfactory? I suggest again my extraordinarily dark and delicate discovery: that it contains things to eat.

The cabbage is a solid; it can be approached from all sides at once; it can be realized by all senses at once. Compared with that the sunflower, which can only be seen, is a mere pattern, a thing painted on a flat wall. Now, it is this sense of the solidity of things that can only be uttered by the metaphor of eating. To express the cubic content of a turnip, you must be all round it at once. The only way to get all round a turnip at once is to eat the turnip. I think any poetic mind that has loved solidity, the thickness of trees, the squareness of stones, the firmness of clay, must have sometimes wished that they were things to eat. If only brown peat tasted as good as it looks; if only white firwood were digestible! We talk rightly of giving stones for bread: but there are in the Geological Museum certain rich crimson marbles, certain split stones of blue and green, that make me wish my teeth were stronger.

Somebody staring into the sky with the same ethereal appetite declared that the moon was made of green cheese. I never could conscientiously accept the full doctrine. I am Modernist in this matter. That the moon is made of cheese I have believed from childhood; and in the course of every month a giant (of my acquaintance) bites a big round piece out of it. This seems to me a doctrine that is above reason, but not contrary to it. But that the cheese is green seems to be in some degree actually contradicted by the senses and the reason; first because if the moon were made of green cheese it would be inhabited; and second because if it were made of green cheese it would be green. A blue moon is said to be an unusual sight; but I cannot think that a green one is much more common. In fact, I think I have seen the moon looking like every other sort of cheese except a green cheese. I have seen it look exactly like a cream cheese: a circle of warm white upon a warm faint violet sky above a cornfield in Kent. I have seen it look very like a Dutch cheese, rising a dull red copper disk amid masts and dark waters at Honfleur. I have seen it look like an ordinary sensible Cheddar cheese in an ordinary sensible Prussian blue sky; and I have once seen it so naked and ruinous-looking, so strangely lit up, that it looked like a Gruyere cheese, that awful volcanic cheese that has horrible holes in it, as if it had come in boiling unnatural milk from mysterious and unearthly cattle. But I have never yet seen the lunar cheese green; and I incline to the opinion that the moon is not old enough. The moon, like everything else, will ripen by the end of the world; and in the last days we shall see it taking on those volcanic sunset colours, and leaping with that enormous and fantastic life.

But this is a parenthesis; and one perhaps slightly lacking in prosaic actuality. Whatever may be the value of the above speculations, the phrase about the moon and green cheese remains a good example of this imagery of eating and drinking on a large scale. The same huge fancy is in the phrase "if all the trees were bread and cheese," which I have cited elsewhere in this connection; and in that noble nightmare of a Scandinavian legend, in which Thor drinks the deep sea nearly dry out of a horn. In an essay like the present (first intended as a paper to be read before the Royal Society) one cannot be too exact; and I will concede that my theory of the gradual vire-scence of our satellite is to be regarded rather as an alternative theory than as a law finally demonstrated and universally accepted by the scientific world. It is a hypothesis that holds the field, as the scientists say of a theory when there is no evidence for it so far.

But the reader need be under no apprehension that I have suddenly gone mad, and shall start biting large pieces out of the trunks of trees; or seriously altering (by large semicircular mouthfuls) the exquisite outline of the mountains. This feeling for expressing a fresh solidity by the image of eating is really a very old one. So far from being a paradox of perversity, it is one of the oldest commonplaces of religion. If any one wandering about wants to have a good trick or test for separating the wrong idealism from the right, I will give him one on the spot. It is a mark of false religion that it is always trying to express concrete facts as abstract; it calls sex affinity; it calls wine alcohol; it calls brute starvation the economic problem. The test of true religion is that its energy drives exactly the other way; it is always trying to make men feel truths as facts; always trying to make abstract things as plain and solid as concrete things; always trying to make men, not merely admit the truth, but see, smell, handle, hear, and devour the truth. All great spiritual scriptures are full of the invitation not to test, but to taste; not to examine, but to eat. Their phrases are full of living water and heavenly bread, mysterious manna and dreadful wine. Worldliness, and the polite society of the world, has despised this instinct of eating; but religion has never despised it. When we look at a firm, fat, white cliff of chalk at Dover, I do not suggest that we should desire to eat it; that would be highly abnormal. But I really mean that we should think it good to eat; good for some one else to eat. For, indeed, some one else is eating it; the grass that grows upon its top is devouring it silently, but, doubtless, with an uproarious appetite.

Simmons and the Social Tie

It is a platitude, and none the less true for that, that we need to have an ideal in our minds with which to test all realities. But it is equally true, and less noted, that we need a reality with which to test ideals. Thus I have selected Mrs. Buttons, a charwoman in Battersea, as the touchstone of all modern theories about the mass of women. Her name is not Buttons; she is not in the least a contemptible nor entirely a comic figure. She has a powerful stoop and an ugly, attractive face, a little like that of Huxley—without the whiskers, of course. The courage with which she supports the most brutal bad luck has something quite creepy about it. Her irony is incessant and inventive; her practical charity very large; and she is wholly unaware of the philosophical use to which I put her.

But when I hear the modern generalization about her sex on all sides I simply substitute her name, and see how the thing sounds then. When on the one side the mere sentimentalist says, "Let woman be content to be dainty and exquisite, a protected piece of social art and domestic ornament," then I merely repeat it to myself in the "other form," "Let Mrs. Buttons be content to be dainty and exquisite, a protected piece of social art, etc." It is extraordinary what a difference the substitution seems to make. And on the other hand, when some of the Suffragettes say in their pamphlets and speeches, "Woman, leaping to life at the trumpet call of Ibsen and Shaw, drops her tawdry luxuries and demands to grasp the sceptre of empire and the firebrand of speculative thought"—in order to understand such a sentence I say it over again in the amended form: "Mrs. Buttons, leaping to life at the trumpet call of Ibsen and Shaw, drops her tawdry luxuries and demands to grasp the sceptre of empire and the firebrand of speculative thought." Somehow it sounds quite different. And yet when you say Woman I suppose you mean the average woman; and if most women are as capable and critical and morally sound as Mrs. Buttons, it is as much as we can expect, and a great deal more than we deserve.

But this study is not about Mrs. Buttons; she would require many studies. I will take a less impressive case of my principle, the principle of keeping in the mind an actual personality when we are talking about types or tendencies or generalized ideals. Take, for example, the question of the education of boys. Almost every post brings me pamphlets expounding some advanced and suggestive scheme of education; the pupils are to be taught separate; the sexes are to be taught together; there should be no prizes; there should be no punishments; the master should lift the boys to his level; the master should descend to their level; we should encourage the heartiest comradeship among boys, and also the tenderest spiritual intimacy with masters; toil must be pleasant and holidays must be instructive; with all these things I am daily impressed and somewhat bewildered. But on the great Buttons' principle I keep in my mind and apply to all these ideals one still vivid fact; the face and character of a particular schoolboy whom I once knew. I am not taking a mere individual oddity, as you will hear. He was exceptional, and yet the reverse of eccentric; he was (in a quite sober and strict sense of the words) exceptionally average. He was the incarnation and the exaggeration of a certain spirit which is the common spirit of boys, but which nowhere else became so obvious and outrageous. And because he was an incarnation he was, in his way, a tragedy.

I will call him Simmons. He was a tall, healthy figure, strong, but a little slouching, and there was in his walk something between a slight swagger and a seaman's roll; he commonly had his hands in his pockets. His hair was dark, straight, and undistinguished; and his face, if one saw it after his figure, was something of a surprise. For while the form might be called big and braggart, the face might have been called weak, and was certainly worried. It was a hesitating face, which seemed to blink doubtfully in the daylight. He had even the look of one who has received a buffet that he cannot return. In all occupations he was the average boy; just sufficiently good at sports, just sufficiently bad at work to be universally satisfactory. But he was prominent in nothing, for prominence was to him a thing like bodily pain. He could not endure, without discomfort amounting to desperation, that any boy should be noticed or sensationally separated from the long line of boys; for him, to be distinguished was to be disgraced.

Those who interpret schoolboys as merely wooden and barbarous, unmoved by anything but a savage seriousness about tuck or cricket, make the mistake of forgetting how much of the schoolboy life is public and ceremonial, having reference to an ideal; or, if you like, to an affectation. Boys, like dogs, have a sort of romantic ritual which is not always their real selves. And this romantic ritual is generally the ritual of not being romantic; the pretence of being much more masculine and materialistic than they are. Boys in themselves are very sentimental. The most sentimental thing in the world is to hide your feelings; it is making too much of them. Stoicism is the direct product of sentimentalism; and schoolboys are sentimental individually, but stoical collectively.

For example, there were numbers of boys at my school besides myself who took a private pleasure in poetry; but red-hot iron would not have induced most of us to admit this to the masters, or to repeat poetry with the faintest inflection of rhythm or intelligence. That would have been anti-social egoism; we called it "showing off." I myself remember running to school (an extraordinary thing to do) with mere internal ecstasy in repeating lines of Walter Scott about the taunts of Marmion or the boasts of Roderick Dhu, and then repeating the same lines in class with the colourless decorum of a hurdy-gurdy. We all wished to be invisible in our uniformity; a mere pattern of Eton collars and coats.

But Simmons went even further. He felt it as an insult to brotherly equality if any task or knowledge out of the ordinary track was discovered even by accident. If a boy had learnt German in infancy; or if a boy knew some terms in music; or if a boy was forced to confess feebly that he had read "The Mill on the Floss"—then Simmons was in a perspiration of discomfort. He felt no personal anger, still less any petty jealousy, what he felt was an honourable and generous shame. He hated it as a lady hates coarseness in a pantomime; it made him want to hide himself. Just that feeling of impersonal ignominy which most of us have when some one betrays indecent ignorance, Simmons had when some one betrayed special knowledge. He writhed and went red in the face; he used to put up the lid of his desk to hide his blushes for human dignity, and from behind this barrier would whisper protests which had the hoarse emphasis of pain. "O, shut up, I say... O, I say, shut up.... O, shut it, can't you?" Once when a little boy admitted that he had heard of the Highland claymore, Simmons literally hid his head inside his desk and dropped the lid upon it in desperation; and when I was for a moment transferred from the bottom of the form for knowing the name of Cardinal Newman, I thought he would have rushed from the room.

His psychological eccentricity increased; if one can call that an eccentricity which was a wild worship of the ordinary. At last he grew so sensitive that he could not even bear any question answered correctly without grief. He felt there was a touch of disloyalty, of unfraternal individualism, even about knowing the right answer to a sum. If asked the date of the battle of Hastings, he considered it due to social tact and general good feeling to answer 1067. This chivalrous exaggeration led to bad feeling between him and the school authority, which ended in a rupture unexpectedly violent in the case of so good-humoured a creature. He fled from the school, and it was discovered upon inquiry that he had fled from his home also.

I never expected to see him again; yet it is one of the two or three odd coincidences of my life that I did see him. At some public sports or recreation ground I saw a group of rather objectless youths, one of whom was wearing the dashing uniform of a private in the Lancers. Inside that uniform was the tall figure, shy face, and dark, stiff hair of Simmons. He had gone to the one place where every one is dressed alike—a regiment. I know nothing more; perhaps he was killed in Africa. But when England was full of flags and false triumphs, when everybody was talking manly trash about the whelps of the lion and the brave boys in red, I often heard a voice echoing in the under-caverns of my memory, "Shut up... O, shut up... O, I say, shut it."

Cheese

My forthcoming work in five volumes, "The Neglect of Cheese in European Literature" is a work of such unprecedented and laborious detail that it is doubtful if I shall live to finish it. Some overflowings from such a fountain of information may therefore be permitted to springle these pages. I cannot yet wholly explain the neglect to which I refer. Poets have been mysteriously silent on the subject of cheese. Virgil, if I remember right, refers to it several times, but with too much Roman restraint. He does not let himself go on cheese. The only other poet I can think of just now who seems to have had some sensibility on the point was the nameless author of the nursery rhyme which says: "If all the trees were bread and cheese"—which is, indeed a rich and gigantic vision of the higher gluttony. If all the trees were bread and cheese there would be considerable deforestation in any part of England where I was living. Wild and wide woodlands would reel and fade before me as rapidly as they ran after Orpheus. Except Virgil and this anonymous rhymer, I can recall no verse about cheese. Yet it has every quality which we require in exalted poetry. It is a short, strong word; it rhymes to "breeze" and "seas" (an essential point); that it is emphatic in sound is admitted even by the civilization of the modern cities. For their citizens, with no apparent intention except emphasis, will often say, "Cheese it!" or even "Quite the cheese." The substance itself is imaginative. It is ancient—sometimes in the individual case, always in the type and custom. It is simple, being directly derived from milk, which is one of the ancestral drinks, not lightly to be corrupted with soda-water. You know, I hope (though I myself have only just thought of it), that the four rivers of Eden were milk, water, wine, and ale. Aerated waters only appeared after the Fall.

But cheese has another quality, which is also the very soul of song. Once in endeavouring to lecture in several places at once, I made an eccentric journey across England, a journey of so irregular and even illogical shape that it necessitated my having lunch on four successive days in four roadside inns in four different counties. In each inn they had nothing but bread and cheese; nor can I imagine why a man should want more than bread and cheese, if he can get enough of it. In each inn the cheese was good; and in each inn it was different. There was a noble Wensleydale cheese in Yorkshire, a Cheshire cheese in Cheshire, and so on. Now, it is just here that true poetic civilization differs from that paltry and mechanical civilization which holds us all in bondage. Bad customs are universal and rigid, like modern militarism. Good customs are universal and varied, like native chivalry and self-defence. Both the good and bad civilization cover us as with a canopy, and protect us from all that is outside. But a good civilization spreads over us freely like a tree, varying and yielding because it is alive. A bad civilization stands up and sticks out above us like an umbrella—artificial, mathematical in shape; not merely universal, but uniform. So it is with the contrast between the substances that vary and the substances that are the same wherever they penetrate. By a wise doom of heaven men were commanded to eat cheese, but not the same cheese. Being really universal it varies from valley to valley. But if, let us say, we compare cheese with soap (that vastly inferior substance), we shall see that soap tends more and more to be merely Smith's Soap or Brown's Soap, sent automatically all over the world. If the Red Indians have soap it is Smith's Soap. If the Grand Lama has soap it is Brown's soap. There is nothing subtly and strangely Buddhist, nothing tenderly Tibetan, about his soap. I fancy the Grand Lama does not eat cheese (he is not worthy), but if he does it is probably a local cheese, having some real relation to his life and outlook. Safety matches, tinned foods, patent medicines are sent all over the world; but they are not produced all over the world. Therefore there is in them a mere dead identity, never that soft play of slight variation which exists in things produced everywhere out of the soil, in the milk of the kine, or the fruits of the orchard. You can get a whisky and soda at every outpost of the Empire: that is why so many Empire-builders go mad. But you are not tasting or touching any environment, as in the cider of Devonshire or the grapes of the Rhine. You are not approaching Nature in one of her myriad tints of mood, as in the holy act of eating cheese.

When I had done my pilgrimage in the four wayside public-houses I reached one of the great northern cities, and there I proceeded, with great rapidity and complete inconsistency, to a large and elaborate restaurant, where I knew I could get many other things besides bread and cheese. I could get that also, however; or at least I expected to get it; but I was sharply reminded that I had entered Babylon, and left England behind. The waiter brought me cheese, indeed, but cheese cut up into contemptibly small pieces; and it is the awful fact that, instead of Christian bread, he brought me biscuits. Biscuits—to one who had eaten the cheese of four great countrysides! Biscuits—to one who had proved anew for himself the sanctity of the ancient wedding between cheese and bread! I addressed the waiter in warm and moving terms. I asked him who he was that he should put asunder those whom Humanity had joined. I asked him if he did not feel, as an artist, that a solid but yielding substance like cheese went naturally with a solid, yielding substance like bread; to eat it off biscuits is like eating it off slates. I asked him if, when he said his prayers, he was so supercilious as to pray for his daily biscuits. He gave me generally to understand that he was only obeying a custom of Modern Society. I have therefore resolved to raise my voice, not against the waiter, but against Modern Society, for this huge and unparalleled modern wrong.

The Red Town

When a man says that democracy is false because most people are stupid, there are several courses which the philosopher may pursue. The most obvious is to hit him smartly and with precision on the exact tip of the nose. But if you have scruples (moral or physical) about this course, you may proceed to employ Reason, which in this case has all the savage solidity of a blow with the fist. It is stupid to say that "most people" are stupid. It is like saying "most people are tall," when it is obvious that "tall" can only mean taller than most people. It is absurd to denounce the majority of mankind as below the average of mankind.

Should the man have been hammered on the nose and brained with logic, and should he still remain cold, a third course opens: lead him by the hand (himself half-willing) towards some sunlit and yet secret meadow and ask him who made the names of the common wild flowers. They were ordinary people, so far as any one knows, who gave to one flower the name of the Star of Bethlehem and to another and much commoner flower the tremendous title of the Eye of Day. If you cling to the snobbish notion that common people are prosaic, ask any common person for the local names of the flowers, names which vary not only from county to county, but even from dale to dale.

But, curiously enough, the case is much stronger than this. It will be said that this poetry is peculiar to the country populace, and that the dim democracies of our modern towns at least have lost it. For some extraordinary reason they have not lost it. Ordinary London slang is full of witty things said by nobody in particular. True, the creed of our cruel cities is not so sane and just as the creed of the old countryside; but the people are just as clever in giving names to their sins in the city as in giving names to their joys in the wilderness. One could not better sum up Christianity than by calling a small white insignificant flower "The Star of Bethlehem." But then, again, one could not better sum up the philosophy deduced from Darwinism than in the one verbal picture of "having your monkey up."

Who first invented these violent felicities of language? Who first spoke of a man "being off his head"? The obvious comment on a lunatic is that his head is off him; yet the other phrase is far more fantastically exact. There is about every madman a singular sensation that his body has walked off and left the important part of him behind.

But the cases of this popular perfection in phrase are even stronger when they are more vulgar. What concentrated irony and imagination there is for instance, in the metaphor which describes a man doing a midnight flitting as "shooting the moon"? It expresses everything about the run away: his eccentric occupation, his improbable explanations, his furtive air as of a hunter, his constant glances at the blank clock in the sky.

No; the English democracy is weak enough about a number of things; for instance, it is weak in politics. But there is no doubt that democracy is wonderfully strong in literature. Very few books that the cultured class has produced of late have been such good literature as the expression "painting the town red."

Oddly enough, this last Cockney epigram clings to my memory. For as I was walking a little while ago round a corner near Victoria I realized for the first time that a familiar lamp-post was painted all over with a bright vermilion just as if it were trying (in spite of the obvious bodily disqualification) to pretend that it was a pillar-box. I have since heard official explanations of these startling and scarlet objects. But my first fancy was that some dissipated gentleman on his way home at four o'clock in the morning had attempted to paint the town red and got only as far as one lamp-post.

I began to make a fairy tale about the man; and, indeed, this phrase contains both a fairy tale and a philosophy; it really states almost the whole truth about those pure outbreaks of pagan enjoyment to which all healthy men have often been tempted. It expresses the desire to have levity on a large scale which is the essence of such a mood. The rowdy young man is not content to paint his tutor's door green: he would like to paint the whole city scarlet. The word which to us best recalls such gigantesque idiocy is the word "mafficking." The slaves of that saturnalia were not only painting the town red; they thought that they were painting the map red—that they were painting the world red. But, indeed, this Imperial debauch has in it something worse than the mere larkiness which is my present topic; it has an element of real self-flattery and of sin. The Jingo who wants to admire himself is worse than the blackguard who only wants to enjoy himself. In a very old ninth-century illumination which I have seen, depicting the war of the rebel angels in heaven, Satan is represented as distributing to his followers peacock feathers—the symbols of an evil pride. Satan also distributed peacock feathers to his followers on Mafeking Night...

But taking the case of ordinary pagan recklessness and pleasure seeking, it is, as we have said, well expressed in this image. First, because it conveys this notion of filling the world with one private folly; and secondly, because of the profound idea involved in the choice of colour. Red is the most joyful and dreadful thing in the physical universe; it is the fiercest note, it is the highest light, it is the place where the walls of this world of ours wear thinnest and something beyond burns through. It glows in the blood which sustains and in the fire which destroys us, in the roses of our romance and in the awful cup of our religion. It stands for all passionate happiness, as in faith or in first love.

Now, the profligate is he who wishes to spread this crimson of conscious joy over everything; to have excitement at every moment; to paint everything red. He bursts a thousand barrels of wine to incarnadine the streets; and sometimes (in his last madness) he will butcher beasts and men to dip his gigantic brushes in their blood. For it marks the sacredness of red in nature, that it is secret even when it is ubiquitous, like blood in the human body, which is omnipresent, yet invisible. As long as blood lives it is hidden; it is only dead blood that we see. But the earlier parts of the rake's progress are very natural and amusing. Painting the town red is a delightful thing until it is done. It would be splendid to see the cross of St. Paul's as red as the cross of St. George, and the gallons of red paint running down the dome or dripping from the Nelson Column. But when it is done, when you have painted the town red, an extraordinary thing happens. You cannot see any red at all.

    I can see, as in a sort of vision, the successful artist standing in the midst of that frightful city, hung on all sides with the scarlet of his shame. And then, when everything is red, he will long for a red rose in a green hedge and long in vain; he will dream of a red leaf and be unable even to imagine it. He has desecrated the divine colour, and he can no longer see it, though it is all around. I see him, a single black figure against the red-hot hell that he has kindled, where spires and turrets stand up like immobile flames: he is stiffened in a sort of agony of prayer. Then the mercy of Heaven is loosened, and I see one or two flakes of snow very slowly begin to fall.

G. K. Chesterton

The Furrows

As I see the corn grow green all about my neighbourhood, there rushes on me for no reason in particular a memory of the winter. I say "rushes," for that is the very word for the old sweeping lines of the ploughed fields. From some accidental turn of a train-journey or a walking tour, I saw suddenly the fierce rush of the furrows. The furrows are like arrows; they fly along an arc of sky. They are like leaping animals; they vault an inviolable hill and roll down the other side. They are like battering battalions; they rush over a hill with flying squadrons and carry it with a cavalry charge. They have all the air of Arabs sweeping a desert, of rockets sweeping the sky, of torrents sweeping a watercourse. Nothing ever seemed so living as those brown lines as they shot sheer from the height of a ridge down to their still whirl of the valley. They were swifter than arrows, fiercer than Arabs, more riotous and rejoicing than rockets. And yet they were only thin straight lines drawn with difficulty, like a diagram, by painful and patient men. The men that ploughed tried to plough straight; they had no notion of giving great sweeps and swirls to the eye. Those cataracts of cloven earth; they were done by the grace of God. I had always rejoiced in them; but I had never found any reason for my joy. There are some very clever people who cannot enjoy the joy unless they understand it. There are other and even cleverer people who say that they lose the joy the moment they do understand it. Thank God I was never clever, and I could always enjoy things when I understood them and when I didn't. I can enjoy the orthodox Tory, though I could never understand him. I can also enjoy the orthodox Liberal, though I understand him only too well.

But the splendour of furrowed fields is this: that like all brave things they are made straight, and therefore they bend. In everything that bows gracefully there must be an effort at stiffness. Bows arc beautiful when they bend only because they try to remain rigid; and sword-blades can curl like silver ribbons only because they are certain to spring straight again. But the same is true of every tough curve of the tree-trunk, of every strong-backed bend of the bough; there is hardly any such thing in Nature as a mere droop of weakness. Rigidity yielding a little, like justice swayed by mercy, is the whole beauty of the earth. The cosmos is a diagram just bent beautifully out of shape. Everything tries to be straight; and everything just fortunately fails.

The foil may curve in the lunge, but there is nothing beautiful about beginning the battle with a crooked foil. So the strict aim, the strong doctrine, may give a little in the actual fight with facts: but that is no reason for beginning with a weak doctrine or a twisted aim. Do not be an opportunist; try to be theoretic at all the opportunities; fate can be trusted to do all the opportunist part of it. Do not try to bend, any more than the trees try to bend. Try to grow straight, and life will bend you.

Alas! I am giving the moral before the fable; and yet I hardly think that otherwise you could see all that I mean in that enormous vision of the

Mrs. Donald F. Donahue

Beginning May 9th
p. 13 - Read at least 3 pp/day.

ploughed hills. These great furrowed slopes are the oldest architecture of man: the oldest astronomy was his guide, the oldest botany his object. And for geometry, the mere word proves my case.

But when I looked at those torrents of ploughed parallels, that great rush of rigid lines, I seemed to see the whole huge achievement of democracy, Here was mere equality: but equality seen in bulk is more superb than any supremacy. Equality free and flying, equality rushing over hill and dale, equality charging the world—that was the meaning of those military furrows, military in their identity, military in their energy. They sculptured hill and dale with strong curves merely because they did not mean to curve at all. They made the strong lines of landscape with their stiffly driven swords of the soil. It is not only nonsense, but blasphemy, to say that man has spoilt the country. Man has created the country; it was his business, as the image of God. No hill, covered with common scrub or patches of purple heath, could have been so sublimely hilly as that ridge up to which the ranked furrows rose like aspiring angels. No valley, confused with needless cottages and towns, can have been so utterly valleyish as that abyss into which the down-rushing furrows raged like demons into the swirling pit.

It is the hard lines of discipline and equality that mark out a landscape and give it all its mould and meaning. It is just because the lines of the furrow arc ugly and even that the landscape is living and superb. As I think I have remarked elsewhere, the Republic is founded on the plough.

G. K. Chesterton

The Philosophy of Sight-seeing

It would be really interesting to know exactly why an intelligent person—by which I mean a person with any sort of intelligence—can and does dislike sight-seeing. Why does the idea of a char-a-banc full of tourists going to see the birth-place of Nelson or the death-scene of Simon de Montfort strike a strange chill to the soul? I can tell quite easily what this dim aversion to tourists and their antiquities does not arise from—at least, in my case. Whatever my other vices (and they are, of course, of a lurid cast), I can lay my hand on my heart and say that it does not arise from a paltry contempt for the antiquities, nor yet from the still more paltry contempt for the tourists. If there is one thing more dwarfish and pitiful than irreverence for the past, it is irreverence for the present, for the passionate and many-coloured procession of life, which includes the char-a-banc among its many chariots and triumphal cars. I know nothing so vulgar as that contempt for vulgarity which sneers at the clerks on a Bank Holiday or the Cockneys on Margate sands. The man who notices nothing about the clerk except his Cockney accent would have noticed nothing about Simon de Montfort except his French accent. The man who jeers at Jones for having dropped an "h" might have jeered at Nelson for having dropped an arm. Scorn springs easily to the essentially vulgar-minded, and it is as easy to gibe at Montfort as a foreigner or at Nelson as a cripple, as to gibe at the struggling speech and the maimed bodies of the mass of our comic and tragic race. If I shrink faintly from this affair of tourists and tombs, it is certainly not because I am so profane as to think lightly either of the tombs or the tourists. I reverence those great men who had the courage to die; I reverence also these little men who have the courage to live.

Even if this be conceded, another suggestion may be made. It may be said that antiquities and commonplace crowds are indeed good things, like violets and geraniums; but they do not go together. A billycock is a beautiful object (it may be eagerly urged), but it is not in the same style of architecture as Ely Cathedral; it is a dome, a small rococo dome in the Renaissance manner, and does not go with the pointed arches that assault heaven like spears. A char-a-banc is lovely (it may be said) if placed upon a pedestal and worshipped for its own sweet sake; but it does not harmonize with the curve and outline of the old three-decker on which Nelson died; its beauty is quite of another sort. Therefore (we will suppose our sage to argue) antiquity and democracy should be kept separate, as inconsistent things. Things may be inconsistent in time and space which are by no means inconsistent in essential value and idea. Thus the Catholic Church has water for the new-born and oil for the dying: but she never mixes oil and water.

This explanation is plausible; but I do not find it adequate. The first objection is that the same smell of bathos haunts the soul in the case of all deliberate and elaborate visits to "beauty spots," even by persons of the most elegant position or the most protected privacy. Specially visiting the Coliseum by moonlight always struck me as being as vulgar as visiting it by limelight. One millionaire standing on the top of Mont Blanc, one millionaire standing in the desert by the Sphinx, one millionaire standing in the middle of Stonehenge, is just as comic as one millionaire is anywhere else; and that is saying a good deal. On the other hand, if the billycock had come privately and naturally into Ely Cathedral, no enthusiast for Gothic harmony would think of objecting to the billycock—so long, of course, as it was not worn on the head. But there is indeed a much deeper objection to this theory of the two incompatible excellences of antiquity and popularity. For the truth is that it has been almost entirely the antiquities that have normally interested the populace; and it has been almost entirely the populace who have systematically preserved the antiquities. The Oldest Inhabitant has always been a clodhopper; I have never heard of his being a gentleman. It is the peasants who preserve all traditions of the sites of battles or the building of churches. It is they who remember, so far as any one remembers, the glimpses of fairies or the graver wonders of saints. In the classes above them the supernatural has been slain by the supercilious. That is a true and tremendous text in Scripture which says that "where there is no vision the people perish." But it is equally true in practice that where there is no people the visions perish.

The idea must be abandoned, then, that this feeling of faint dislike towards popular sight-seeing is due to any inherent incompatibility between the idea of special shrines and trophies and the idea of large masses of ordinary men. On the contrary, these two elements of sanctity and democracy have been specially connected and allied throughout history. The shrines and trophies were often put up by ordinary men. They were always put up for ordinary men. To whatever things the fastidious modern artist may choose to apply his theory of specialist judgment, and an aristocracy of taste, he must necessarily find it difficult really to apply it to such historic and monumental art. Obviously, a public building is meant to impress the public. The most aristocratic tomb is a democratic tomb, because it exists to be seen; the only aristocratic thing is the decaying corpse, not the undecaying marble; and if the man wanted to be thoroughly aristocratic, he should be buried in his own back-garden. The chapel of the most narrow and exclusive sect is universal outside, even if it is limited inside, its walls and windows confront all points of the compass and all quarters of the cosmos. It may be small as a dwelling-place, but it is universal as a monument; if its sectarians had really wished to be private they should have met in a private house. Whenever and wherever we erect a national or municipal hall, pillar, or statue, we are speaking to the crowd like a demagogue.

The statue of every statesman offers itself for election as much as the statesman himself. Every epitaph on a church slab is put up for the mob as much as a placard in a General Election. And if we follow this track of reflection we shall, I think, really find why it is that modern sight-seeing jars on something in us, something that is not a caddish contempt for graves nor an equally caddish contempt for cads. For, after all, there is many a—churchyard which consists mostly of dead cads; but that does not make it less sacred or less sad.

The real explanation, I fancy, is this: that these cathedrals and columns of triumph were meant, not for people more cultured and self-conscious than modern tourists, but for people much rougher and more casual. Those leaps of live stone like frozen fountains, were so placed and poised as to catch the eye of ordinary inconsiderate men going about their daily business; and when they are so seen they are never forgotten. The true way of reviving the magic of our great minsters and historic sepulchres is not the one which Ruskin was always recommending. It is not to be more careful of historic buildings. Nay, it is rather to be more careless of them. Buy a bicycle in Maidstone to visit an aunt in Dover, and you will see Canterbury Cathedral as it was built to be seen. Go through London only as the shortest way between Croydon and Hampstead, and the Nelson Column will (for the first time in your life) remind you of Nelson. You will appreciate Hereford Cathedral if you have come for cider, not if you have come for architecture. You will really see the Place Vendome if you have come on business, not if you have come for art. For it was for the simple and laborious generations of men, practical, troubled about many things, that our fathers reared those portents. There is, indeed, another element, not unimportant: the fact that people have gone to cathedrals to pray. But in discussing modern artistic cathedral-lovers, we need not consider this.

A Criminal Head

When men of science (or, more often, men who talk about science) speak of studying history or human society scientifically they always forget that there are two quite distinct questions involved. It may be that certain facts of the body go with certain facts of the soul, but it by no means follows that a grasp of such facts of the body goes with a grasp of the things of the soul. A man may show very learnedly that certain mixtures of race make a happy community, but he may be quite wrong (he generally is) about what communities are happy. A man may explain scientifically how a certain physical type involves a really bad man, but he may be quite wrong (he generally is) about which sort of man is really bad. Thus his whole argument is useless, for he understands only one half of the equation.

The drearier kind of don may come to me and say, "Celts are unsuccessful; look at Irishmen, for instance." To which I should reply, "You may know all about Celts; but it is obvious that you know nothing about Irishmen. The Irish are not in the least unsuccessful, unless it is unsuccessful to wander from their own country over a great part of the earth, in which case the English are unsuccessful too." A man with a bumpy head may say to me (as a kind of New Year greeting), "Fools have microcephalous skulls," or what not. To which I shall reply, "In order to be certain of that, you must be a good judge both of the physical and of the mental fact. It is not enough that you should know a microcephalous skull when you see it. It is also necessary that you should know a fool when you see him; and I have a suspicion that you do not know a fool when you see him, even after the most lifelong and intimate of all forms of acquaintanceship."

The trouble with most sociologists, criminologists, etc., is that while their knowledge of their own details is exhaustive and subtle, their knowledge of man and society, to which these are to be applied, is quite exceptionally superficial and silly. They know everything about biology, but almost nothing about life. Their ideas of history, for instance, are simply cheap and uneducated. Thus some famous and foolish professor measured the skull of Charlotte Corday to ascertain the criminal type; he had not historical knowledge enough to know that if there is any "criminal type," certainly Charlotte Corday had not got it. The skull, I believe, afterwards turned out not to be Charlotte Corday's at all; but that is another story. The point is that the poor old man was trying to match Charlotte Corday's mind with her skull without knowing anything whatever about her mind.

But I came yesterday upon a yet more crude and startling example.

In a popular magazine there is one of the usual articles about criminology; about whether wicked men could be made good if their heads were taken to pieces. As by far the wickedest men I know of are much too rich and powerful ever to submit to the process, the speculation leaves me cold. I always notice with pain, however, a curious absence of the portraits of living millionaires from such galleries of awful examples; most of the portraits in which we are called upon to remark the line of the nose or the curve of the forehead appear to be the portraits of ordinary sad men, who stole because they were hungry or killed because they were in a rage. The physical peculiarity seems to vary infinitely; sometimes it is the remarkable square head, sometimes it is the unmistakable round head; sometimes the learned draw attention to the abnormal development, sometimes to the striking deficiency of the back of the head. I have tried to discover what is the invariable factor, the one permanent mark of the scientific criminal type; after exhaustive classification I have to come to the conclusion that it consists in being poor.

But it was among the pictures in this article that I received the final shock; the enlightenment which has left me in lasting possession of the fact that criminologists are generally more ignorant than criminals. Among the starved and bitter, but quite human, faces was one head, neat but old-fashioned, with the powder of the 18th century and a certain almost pert primness in the dress which marked the conventions of the upper middle-class about 1790. The face was lean and lifted stiffly up, the eyes stared forward with a frightful sincerity, the lip was firm with a heroic firmness; all the more pathetic because of a certain delicacy and deficiency of male force, Without knowing who it was, one could have guessed that it was a man in the manner of Shakespeare's Brutus, a man of piercingly pure intentions, prone to use government as a mere machine for morality, very sensitive to the charge of inconsistency and a little too proud of his own clean and honourable life. I say I should have known this almost from the face alone, even if I had not known who it was.

But I did know who it was. It was Robespierre. And underneath the portrait of this pale and too eager moralist were written these remarkable words: "Deficiency of ethical instincts," followed by something to the effect that he knew no mercy (which is certainly untrue), and by some nonsense about a retreating forehead, a peculiarity which he shared with Louis XVI and with half the people of his time and ours.

Then it was that I measured the staggering distance between the knowledge and the ignorance of science. Then I knew that all criminology might be worse than worthless, because of its utter ignorance of that human material of which it is supposed to be speaking. The man who could say that Robespierre was deficient in ethical instincts is a man utterly to be disregarded in all calculations of ethics. He might as well say that John Bunyan was deficient in ethical instincts. You may say that Robespierre was morbid and unbalanced, and you may say the same of Bunyan. But if these two men were morbid and unbalanced they were morbid and unbalanced by feeling too much about morality, not by feeling too little. You may say if you like that Robespierre was (in a negative sort of way) mad. But if he was mad he was mad on ethics. He and a company of keen and pugnacious men, intellectually impatient of unreason and wrong, resolved that Europe should not be choked up in every channel by oligarchies and state secrets that already stank. The work was the greatest that was ever given to men to do except that which Christianity did in dragging Europe out of the abyss of barbarism after the Dark Ages. But they did it, and no one else could have done it.

Certainly we could not do it. We are not ready to fight all Europe on a point of justice. We are not ready to fling our most powerful class as mere refuse to the foreigner; we are not ready to shatter the great estates at a stroke; we are not ready to trust ourselves in an awful moment of utter dissolution in order to make all things seem intelligible and all men feel honourable henceforth. We are not strong enough to be as strong as Danton. We are not strong enough to be as weak as Robespierre. There is only one thing, it seems, that we can do. Like a mob of children, we can play games upon this ancient battlefield; we can pull up the bones and skulls of the tyrants and martyrs of that unimaginable war; and we can chatter to each other childishly and innocently about skulls that are imbecile and heads that are criminal. I do not know whose heads are criminal, but I think I know whose are imbecile.

G. K. Chesterton

The Wrath of the Roses

The position of the rose among flowers is like that of the dog among animals. It is so much that both are domesticated as that have some dim feeling that they were always domesticated. There are wild roses and there are wild dogs. I do not know the wild dogs; wild roses are very nice. But nobody ever thinks of either of them if the name is abruptly mentioned in a gossip or a poem. On the other hand, there are tame tigers and tame cobras, but if one says, "I have a cobra in my pocket," or "There is a tiger in the music-room," the adjective "tame" has to be somewhat hastily added. If one speaks of beasts one thinks first of wild beasts; if of flowers one thinks first of wild flowers.

But there are two great exceptions; caught so completely into the wheel of man's civilization, entangled so unalterably with his ancient emotions and images, that the artificial product seems more natural than the natural. The dog is not a part of natural history, but of human history; and the real rose grows in a garden. All must regard the elephant as something tremendous, but tamed; and many, especially in our great cultured centres, regard every bull as presumably a mad bull. In the same way we think of most garden trees and plants as fierce creatures of the forest or morass taught at last to endure the curb.

But with the dog and the rose this instinctive principle is reversed. With them we think of the artificial as the archetype; the earth-born as the erratic exception. We think vaguely of the wild dog as if he had run away, like the stray cat. And we cannot help fancying that the wonderful wild rose of our hedges has escaped by jumping over the hedge. Perhaps they fled together, the dog and the rose: a singular and (on the whole) an imprudent elopement. Perhaps the treacherous dog crept from the kennel, and the rebellious rose from the flower-bed, and they fought their way out in company, one with teeth and the other with thorns. Possibly this is why my dog becomes a wild dog when he sees roses, and kicks them anywhere. Possibly this is why the wild rose is called a dog-rose. Possibly not.

But there is this degree of dim barbaric truth in the quaint old-world legend that I have just invented. That in these two cases the civilized product is felt to be the fiercer, nay, even the wilder. Nobody seems to be afraid of a wild dog: he is classed among the jackals and the servile beasts. The terrible cave canem is written over man's creation. When we read "Beware of the Dog," it means beware of the tame dog: for it is the tame dog that is terrible. He is terrible in proportion as he is tame: it is his loyalty and his virtues that are awful to the stranger, even the stranger within your gates; still more to the stranger halfway over your gates. He is alarmed at such deafening and furious docility; he flees from that great monster of mildness.

Well, I have much the same feeling when I look at the roses ranked red and thick and resolute round a garden; they seem to me bold and even blustering. I hasten to say that I know even less about my own garden than about anybody else's garden. I know nothing about roses, not even their names. I know only the name Rose; and Rose is (in every sense of the word) a Christian name. It is Christian in the one absolute and primordial sense of Christian—that it comes down from the age of pagans. The rose can be seen, and even smelt, in Greek, Latin, Provencal, Gothic, Renascence, and Puritan poems. Beyond this mere word Rose, which (like wine and other noble words) is the same in all the tongues of white men, I know literally nothing. I have heard the more evident and advertised names. I know there is a flower which calls itself the Glory of Dijon—which I had supposed to be its cathedral. In any case, to have produced a rose and a cathedral is to have produced not only two very glorious and humane things, but also (as I maintain) two very soldierly and defiant things. I also know there is a rose called Marechal Niel—note once more the military ring.

And when I was walking round my garden the other day I spoke to my gardener (an enterprise of no little valour) and asked him the name of a strange dark rose that had somehow oddly taken my fancy. It was almost as if it reminded me of some turbid element in history and the soul. Its red was not only swarthy, but smoky; there was something congested and wrathful about its colour. It was at once theatrical and sulky. The gardener told me it was called Victor Hugo.

Therefore it is that I feel all roses to have some secret power about them; even their names may mean something in connexion with themselves, in which they differ from nearly all the sons of men. But the rose itself is royal and dangerous; long as it has remained in the rich house of civilization, it has never laid off its armour. A rose always looks like a mediaeval gentleman of Italy, with a cloak of crimson and a sword: for the thorn is the sword of the rose.

And there is this real moral in the matter; that we have to remember that civilization as it goes on ought not perhaps to grow more fighting—but ought to grow more ready to fight. The more valuable and reposeful is the order we have to guard, the more vivid should be our ultimate sense of vigilance and potential violence. And when I walk round a summer garden, I can understand how those high mad lords at the end of the Middle Ages, just before their swords clashed, caught at roses for their instinctive emblems of empire and rivalry. For to me any such garden is full of the wars of the roses.

G. K. Chesterton

The Gold of Glastonbury

One silver morning I walked into a small grey town of stone, like twenty other grey western towns, which happened to be called Glastonbury; and saw the magic thorn of near two thousand years growing in the open air as casually as any bush in my garden.

In Glastonbury, as in all noble and humane things, the myth is more important than the history. One cannot say anything stronger of the strange old tale of St. Joseph and the Thorn than that it dwarfs St. Dunstan. Standing among the actual stones and shrubs one thinks of the first century and not of the tenth; one's mind goes back beyond the Saxons and beyond the greatest statesman of the Dark Ages. The tale that Joseph of Arimathea came to Britain is presumably a mere legend. But it is not by any means so incredible or preposterous a legend as many modern people suppose. The popular notion is that the thing is quite comic and inconceivable; as if one said that Wat Tyler went to Chicago, or that John Bunyan discovered the North Pole. We think of Palestine as little, localized and very private, of Christ's followers as poor folk, astricti globis, rooted to their towns or trades; and we think of vast routes of travel and constant world-communications as things of recent and scientific origin. But this is wrong; at least, the last part of it is. It is part of that large and placid lie that the rationalists tell when they say that Christianity arose in ignorance and barbarism. Christianity arose in the thick of a brilliant and bustling cosmopolitan civilization. Long sea-voyages were not so quick, but were quite as incessant as to-day; and though in the nature of things Christ had not many rich followers, it is not unnatural to suppose that He had some. And a Joseph of Arimathea may easily have been a Roman citizen with a yacht that could visit Britain. The same fallacy is employed with the same partisan motive in the case of the Gospel of St. John; which critics say could not have been written by one of the first few Christians because of its Greek transcendentalism and its Platonic tone. I am no judge of the philology, but every human being is a divinely appointed judge of the philosophy: and the Platonic tone seems to me to prove nothing at all. Palestine was not a secluded valley of barbarians; it was an open province of a polyglot empire, overrun with all sorts of people of all kinds of education. To take a rough parallel: suppose some great prophet arose among the Boers in South Africa. The prophet himself might be a simple or unlettered man. But no one who knows the modern world would be surprised if one of his closest followers were a Professor from Heidelberg or an M.A. from Oxford.

All this is not urged here with any notion of proving that the tale of the thorn is not a myth; as I have said, it probably is a myth. It is urged with the much more important object of pointing out the proper attitude towards such myths.. The proper attitude is one of doubt and hope and of a kind of light mystery. The tale is certainly not impossible; as it is certainly not certain. And through all the ages since the Roman Empire men have fed their healthy fancies and their historical imagination upon the very twilight condition of such tales. But to-day real agnosticism has declined along with real theology. People cannot leave a creed alone; though it is the essence of a creed to be clear. But neither can they leave a legend alone; though it is the essence of a legend to be vague. That sane half scepticism which was found in all rustics, in all ghost tales and fairy tales, seems to be a lost secret. Modern people must make scientifically certain that St. Joseph did or did not go to Glastonbury, despite the fact that it is now quite impossible to find out; and that it does not, in a religious sense, very much matter. But it is essential to feel that he may have gone to Glastonbury: all songs, arts, and dedications branching and blossoming like the thorn, are rooted in some such sacred doubt. Taken thus, not heavily like a problem but lightly like an old tale, the thing does lead one along the road of very strange realities, and the thorn is found growing in the heart of a very secret maze of the soul. Something is really present in the place; some closer contact with the thing which covers Europe but is still a secret. Somehow the grey town and the green bush touch across the world the strange small country of the garden and the grave; there is verily some communion between the thorn tree and the crown of thorns.

    A man never knows what tiny thing will startle him to such ancestral and impersonal tears. Piles of superb masonry will often pass like a common panorama; and on this grey and silver morning the ruined towers of the cathedral stood about me somewhat vaguely like grey clouds. But down in a hollow where the local antiquaries are making a fruitful excavation, a magnificent old ruffian with a pickaxe (whom I believe to have been St. Joseph of Arimathea) showed me a fragment of the old vaulted roof which he had found in the earth; and on the whitish grey stone there was just a faint brush of gold. There seemed a piercing and swordlike pathos, an unexpected fragrance of all forgotten or desecrated things, in the bare survival of that poor little pigment upon the imperishable rock. To the strong shapes of the Roman and the Gothic I had grown accustomed; but that weak touch of colour was at once tawdry and tender, like some popular keepsake. Then I knew that all my fathers were men like me; for the columns and arches were grave, and told of the gravity of the builders; but here was one touch of their gaiety. I almost expected it to fade from the stone as I stared. It was as if men had been able to preserve a fragment of a sunset.

    And then I remembered how the artistic critics have always praised the grave tints and the grim shadows of the crumbling cloisters and abbey towers, and how they themselves often dress up like Gothic ruins in the sombre tones of dim grey walls or dark green ivy. I remembered how they hated almost all primary things, but especially primary colours. I knew they were appreciating much more delicately and truly than I the sublime skeleton and the mighty fungoids of the dead Glastonbury. But I stood for an instant alive in the living Glastonbury, gay with gold and coloured like the toy-book of a child.

G. K. Chesterton

The Futurists

It was a warm golden evening, fit for October, and I was watching (with regret) a lot of little black pigs being turned out of my garden, when the postman handed to me, with a perfunctory haste which doubtless masked his emotion, the Declaration of Futurism. If you ask me what Futurism is, I cannot tell you; even the Futurists themselves seem a little doubtful; perhaps they are waiting for the future to find out. But if you ask me what its Declaration is, I answer eagerly; for I can tell you quite a lot about that. It is written by an Italian named Marinetti, in a magazine which is called Poesia. It is headed "Declaration of Futurism" in enormous letters; it is divided off with little numbers; and it starts straight away like this: "1. We intend to glorify the love of danger, the custom of energy, the strengt of daring. 2. The essential elements of our poetry will be courage, audacity, and revolt. 3. Literature having up to now glorified thoughtful immobility, ecstasy, and slumber, we wish to exalt the aggressive movement, the feverish insomnia, running, the perilous leap, the cuff and the blow." While I am quite willing to exalt the cuff within reason, it scarcely seems such an entirely new subject for literature as the Futurists imagine. It seems to me that even through the slumber which fills the Siege of Troy, the Song of Roland, and the Orlando Furioso, and in spite of the thoughtful immobility which marks "Pantagruel," "Henry V," and the Ballad of Chevy Chase, there are occasional gleams of an admiration for courage, a readiness to glorify the love of danger, and even the "strengt of daring," I seem to remember, slightly differently spelt, somewhere in literature.

The distinction, however, seems to be that the warriors of the past went in for tournaments, which were at least dangerous for themselves, while the Futurists go in for motor-cars, which are mainly alarming for other people. It is the Futurist in his motor who does the "aggressive movement," but it is the pedestrians who go in for the "running" and the "perilous leap." Section No. 4 says, "We declare that the splendour of the world has been enriched with a new form of beauty, the beauty of speed. A race-automobile adorned with great pipes like serpents with explosive breath.... A race-automobile which seems to rush over exploding powder is more beautiful than the Victory of Samothrace." It is also much easier, if you have the money. It is quite clear, however, that you cannot be a Futurist at all unless you are frightfully rich. Then follows this lucid and soul-stirring sentence: "5. We will sing the praises of man holding the flywheel of which the ideal steering-post traverses the earth impelled itself around the circuit of its own orbit." What a jolly song it would be—so hearty, and with such a simple swing in it! I can imagine the Futurists round the fire in a tavern trolling out in chorus some ballad with that incomparable refrain; shouting over their swaying flagons some such words as these:

Alarms and Discursions

A notion came into my head as new as it was bright That poems might be written on the subject of a fight; No praise was given to Lancelot, Achilles, Nap or Corbett, But we will sing the praises of man holding the flywheel of which the ideal steering-post traverses the earth impelled itself around the circuit of its own orbit.

Then lest it should be supposed that Futurism would be so weak as to permit any democratic restraints upon the violence and levity of the luxurious classes, there would be a special verse in honour of the motors also:

My fathers scaled the mountains in their pilgrimages far, But I feel full of energy while sitting in a car; And petrol is the perfect wine, I lick it and absorb it, So we will sing the praises of man holding the flywheel of which the ideal steering-post traverses the earth impelled itself around the circuit of its own orbit.

Yes, it would be a rollicking catch. I wish there were space to finish the song, or to detail all the other sections in the Declaration. Suffice it to say that Futurism has a gratifying dislike both of Liberal politics and Christian morals; I say gratifying because, however unfortunately the cross and the cap of liberty have quarrelled, they are always united in the feeble hatred of such silly megalomaniacs as these. They will "glorify war—the only true hygiene of the world—militarism, patriotism, the destructive gesture of Anarchism, the beautiful ideas which kill, and the scorn of woman." They will "destroy museums, libraries, and fight against moralism, feminism, and all utilitarian cowardice." The proclamation ends with an extraordinary passage which I cannot understand at all, all about something that is going to happen to Mr. Marinetti when he is forty. As far as I can make out he will then be killed by other poets, who will be overwhelmed with love and admiration for him. "They will come against us from far away, from everywhere, leaping on the cadence of their first poems, clawing the air with crooked fingers and scenting at the Academy gates the good smell of our decaying minds." Well, it is satisfactory to be told, however obscurely, that this sort of thing is coming to an end some day, to be replaced by some other tomfoolery. And though I commonly refrain from clawing the air with crooked fingers, I can assure Mr. Marinetti that this omission does not disqualify me, and that I scent the good smell of his decaying mind all right.

I think the only other point of Futurism is contained in this sentence: "It is in Italy that we hurl this overthrowing and inflammatory Declaration, with which to-day we found Futurism, for we will free Italy from her numberless museums which cover her with countless cemeteries." I think that rather sums it up. The best way, one would think, of freeing oneself from a museum would be not to go there. Mr. Marinetti's fathers and grandfathers freed Italy from prisons and torture chambers, places where people were held by force. They, being in the bondage of "moralism," attacked Governments as unjust, real Governments, with real guns. Such was their utilitarian cowardice that they would die in hundreds upon the bayonets of Austria. I can well imagine why Mr. Marinetti in his motor-car does not wish to look back at the past. If there was one thing that could make him look smaller even than before it is that roll of dead men's drums and that dream of Garibaldi going by. The old Radical ghosts go by, more real than the living men, to assault I know not what ramparted city in hell. And meanwhile the Futurist stands outside a museum in a warlike attitude, and defiantly tells the official at the turnstile that he will never, never come in.

There is a certain solid use in fools. It is not so much that they rush in where angels fear to tread, but rather that they let out what devils intend to do. Some perversion of folly will float about nameless and pervade a whole society; then some lunatic gives it a name, and henceforth it is harmless. With all really evil things, when the danger has appeared the danger is over. Now it may be hoped that the self-indulgent sprawlers of Poesia have put a name once and for all to their philosophy. In the case of their philosophy, to put a name to it is to put an end to it. Yet their philosophy has been very widespread in our time; it could hardly have been pointed and finished except by this perfect folly. The creed of which (please God) this is the flower and finish consists ultimately in this statement: that it is bold and spirited to appeal to the future. Now, it is entirely weak and half-witted to appeal to the future. A brave man ought to ask for what he wants, not for what he expects to get. A brave man who wants Atheism in the future calls himself an Atheist; a brave man who wants Socialism, a Socialist; a brave man who wants Catholicism, a Catholic. But a weak-minded man who does not know what he wants in the future calls himself a Futurist.

They have driven all the pigs away. Oh that they had driven away the prigs, and left the pigs! The sky begins to droop with darkness and all birds and blossoms to descend unfaltering into the healthy underworld where things slumber and grow. There was just one true phrase of Mr. Marinetti's about himself: "the feverish insomnia." The whole universe is pouring headlong to the happiness of the night. It is only the madman who has not the courage to sleep.

Dukes

The Duc de Chambertin-Pommard was a small but lively relic of a really aristocratic family, the members of which were nearly all Atheists up to the time of the French Revolution, but since that event (beneficial in such various ways) had been very devout. He was a Royalist, a Nationalist, and a perfectly sincere patriot in that particular style which consists of ceaselessly asserting that one's country is not so much in danger as already destroyed. He wrote cheery little articles for the Royalist Press entitled "The End of France" or "The Last Cry," or what not, and he gave the final touches to a picture of the Kaiser riding across a pavement of prostrate Parisians with a glow of patriotic exultation. He was quite poor, and even his relations had no money. He walked briskly to all his meals at a little open cafe, and he looked just like everybody else.

Living in a country where aristocracy does not exist, he had a high opinion of it. He would yearn for the swords and the stately manners of the Pommards before the Revolution—most of whom had been (in theory) Republicans. But he turned with a more practical eagerness to the one country in Europe where the tricolour has never flown and men have never been roughly equalized before the State. The beacon and comfort of his life was England, which all Europe sees clearly as the one pure aristocracy that remains. He had, moreover, a mild taste for sport and kept an English bulldog, and he believed the English to be a race of bulldogs, of heroic squires, and hearty yeomen vassals, because he read all this in English Conservative papers, written by exhausted little Levantine clerks. But his reading was naturally for the most part in the French Conservative papers (though he knew English well), and it was in these that he first heard of the horrible Budget. There he read of the confiscatory revolution planned by the Lord Chancellor of the Exchequer, the sinister Georges Lloyd. He also read how chivalrously Prince Arthur Balfour of Burleigh had defied that demagogue, assisted by Austen the Lord Chamberlain and the gay and witty Walter Lang. And being a brisk partisan and a capable journalist, he decided to pay England a special visit and report to his paper upon the struggle.

He drove for an eternity in an open fly through beautiful woods, with a letter of introduction in his pocket to one duke, who was to introduce him to another duke. The endless and numberless avenues of bewildering pine woods gave him a queer feeling that he was driving through the countless corridors of a dream. Yet the vast silence and freshness healed his irritation at modern ugliness and unrest. It seemed a background fit for the return of chivalry. In such a forest a king and all his court might lose themselves hunting or a knight errant might perish with no companion but God. The castle itself when he reached it was somewhat smaller than he had expected, but he was delighted with its romantic and castellated outline. He was just about to alight when somebody opened two enormous gates at the side and the vehicle drove briskly through.

G. K. Chesterton

"That is not the house?" he inquired politely of the driver.

"No, sir," said the driver, controlling the corners of his mouth. "The lodge, sir."

"Indeed," said the Duc de Chambertin-Pommard, "that is where the Duke's land begins?"

"Oh no, sir," said the man, quite in distress. "We've been in his Grace's land all day."

The Frenchman thanked him and leant back in the carriage, feeling as if everything were incredibly huge and vast, like Gulliver in the country of the Brobdingnags.

He got out in front of a long facade of a somewhat severe building, and a little careless man in a shooting jacket and knickerbockers ran down the steps. He had a weak, fair moustache and dull, blue, babyish eyes; his features were insignificant, but his manner extremely pleasant and hospitable, This was the Duke of Aylesbury, perhaps the largest landowner in Europe, and known only as a horsebreeder until he began to write abrupt little letters about the Budget. He led the French Duke upstairs, talking trivialties in a hearty way, and there presented him to another and more important English oligarch, who got up from a writing-desk with a slightly senile jerk. He had a gleaming bald head and glasses; the lower part of his face was masked with a short, dark beard, which did not conceal a beaming smile, not unmixed with sharpness. He stooped a little as he ran, like some sedentary head clerk or cashier; and even without the cheque-book and papers on his desk would have given the impression of a merchant or man of business. He was dressed in a light grey check jacket. He was the Duke of Windsor, the great Unionist statesman. Between these two loose, amiable men, the little Gaul stood erect in his black frock coat, with the monstrous gravity of French ceremonial good manners. This stiffness led the Duke of Windsor to put him at his ease (like a tenant), and he said, rubbing his hands:

"I was delighted with your letter... delighted. I shall be very pleased if I can give you—er—any details."

"My visit," said the Frenchman, "scarcely suffices for the scientific exhaustion of detail. I seek only the idea. The idea, that is always the immediate thing."

"Quite so," said the other rapidly; "quite so... the idea."

Feeling somehow that it was his turn (the English Duke having done all that could be required of him) Pommard had to say: "I mean the idea of aristocracy. I regard this as the last great battle for the idea. Aristocracy, like any other thing, must justify itself to mankind. Aristocracy is good because it preserves a picture of human dignity in a world where that dignity is often obscured by servile necessities. Aristocracy alone can keep a certain high reticence of soul and body, a certain noble distance between the sexes."

The Duke of Aylesbury, who had a clouded recollection of having squirted soda-water down the neck of a Countess on the previous evening, looked somewhat gloomy, as if lamenting the theoretic spirit of the Latin race. The elder Duke laughed heartily, and said: "Well, well, you know; we English are horribly practical. With us the great question is the land. Out here in the country ... do you know this part?"

"Yes, yes," cried the Frenchmen eagerly. "I See what you mean. The country! the old rustic life of humanity! A holy war upon the bloated and filthy towns. What right have these anarchists to attack your busy and prosperous countrysides? Have they not thriven under your management? Are not the English villages always growing larger and gayer under the enthusiastic leadership of their encouraging squires? Have you not the Maypole? Have you not Merry England?"

The Duke of Aylesbury made a noise in his throat, and then said very indistinctly: "They all go to London."

"All go to London?" repeated Pommard, with a blank stare. "Why?"

This time nobody answered, and Pommard had to attack again.

"The spirit of aristocracy is essentially opposed to the greed of the industrial cities. Yet in France there are actually one or two nobles so vile as to drive coal and gas trades, and drive them hard." The Duke of Windsor looked at the carpet. The Duke of Aylesbury went and looked out of the window. At length the latter said: "That's rather stiff, you know. One has to look after one's own business in town as well."

"Do not say it," cried the little Frenchman, starting up. "I tell you all Europe is one fight between business and honour. If we do not fight for honour, who will? What other right have we poor two-legged sinners to titles and quartered shields except that we staggeringly support some idea of giving things which cannot be demanded and avoiding things which cannot be punished? Our only claim is to be a wall across Christendom against the Jew pedlars and pawnbrokers, against the Goldsteins and the—"

The Duke of Aylesbury swung round with his hands in his pockets.

"Oh, I say," he said, "you've been readin' Lloyd George. Nobody but dirty Radicals can say a word against Goldstein."

"I certainly cannot permit," said the elder Duke, rising rather shakily, "the respected name of Lord Goldstein—"

He intended to be impressive, but there was something in the Frenchman's eye that is not so easily impressed; there shone there that steel which is the mind of France.

"Gentlemen," he said, "I think I have all the details now. You have ruled England for four hundred years. By your own account you have not made the countryside endurable to men. By your own account you have helped the victory of vulgarity and smoke. And by your own account you are hand and glove with those very money-grubbers and adventurers whom gentlemen have no other business but to keep at bay. I do not know what your people will do; but my people would kill you."

Some seconds afterwards he had left the Duke's house, and some hours afterwards the Duke's estate.

G. K. Chesterton

The Glory of Grey

I suppose that, taking this summer as a whole, people will not call it an appropriate time for praising the English climate. But for my part I will praise the English climate till I die—even if I die of the English climate. There is no weather so good as English weather. Nay, in a real sense there is no weather at all anywhere but in England. In France you have much sun and some rain; in Italy you have hot winds and cold winds; in Scotland and Ireland you have rain, either thick or thin; in America you have hells of heat and cold, and in the Tropics you have sunstrokes varied by thunderbolts. But all these you have on a broad and brutal scale, and you settle down into contentment or despair. Only in our own romantic country do you have the strictly romantic thing called Weather; beautiful and changing as a woman. The great English landscape painters (neglected now like everything that is English) have this salient distinction: that the Weather is not the atmosphere of their pictures; it is the subject of their pictures. They paint portraits of the Weather. The Weather sat to Constable. The Weather posed for Turner, and a deuce of a pose it was. This cannot truly be said of the greatest of their continental models or rivals. Poussin and Claude painted objects, ancient cities or perfect Arcadian shepherds through a clear medium of the climate. But in the English painters Weather is the hero; with Turner an Adelphi hero, taunting, flashing and fighting, melodramatic but really magnificent. The English climate, a tall and terrible protagonist, robed in rain and thunder and snow and sunlight, fills the whole canvas and the whole foreground. I admit the superiority of many other French things besides French art. But I will not yield an inch on the superiority of English weather and weather-painting. Why, the French have not even got a word for Weather: and you must ask for the weather in French as if you were asking for the time in English.

Then, again, variety of climate should always go with stability of abode. The weather in the desert is monotonous; and as a natural consequence the Arabs wander about, hoping it may be different somewhere. But an Englishman's house is not only his castle; it is his fairy castle. Clouds and colours of every varied dawn and eve are perpetually touching and turning it from clay to gold, or from gold to ivory. There is a line of woodland beyond a corner of my garden which is literally different on every one of the three hundred and sixty-five days. Sometimes it seems as near as a hedge, and sometimes as far as a faint and fiery evening cloud. The same principle (by the way) applies to the difficult problem of wives. Variability is one of the virtues of a woman. It avoids the crude requirement of polygamy. So long as you have one good wife you are sure to have a spiritual harem.

Now, among the heresies that are spoken in this matter is the habit of calling a grey day a "colourless" day. Grey is a colour, and can be a very powerful and pleasing colour. There is also an insulting style of speech about "one grey day just like another" You might as well talk about one green tree just like another. A grey clouded sky is indeed a canopy between us and the sun; so is a green tree, if it comes to that. But the grey umbrellas differ as much as the green in their style and shape, in their tint and tilt. One day may be grey like steel, and another grey like dove's plumage. One may seem grey like the deathly frost, and another grey like the smoke of substantial kitchens. No things could seem further apart than the doubt of grey and the decision of scarlet. Yet grey and red can mingle, as they do in the morning clouds: and also in a sort of warm smoky stone of which they build the little towns in the west country. In those towns even the houses that are wholly grey have a glow in them; as if their secret firesides were such furnaces of hospitality as faintly to transfuse the walls like walls of cloud. And wandering in those westland parts I did once really find a signpost pointing up a steep crooked path to a town that was called Clouds. I did not climb up to it; I feared that either the town would not be good enough for the name, or I should not be good enough for the town. Anyhow, the little hamlets of the warm grey stone have a geniality which is not achieved by all the artistic scarlet of the suburbs; as if it were better to warm one's hands at the ashes of Glastonbury than at the painted flames of Croydon.

    Again, the enemies of grey (those astute, daring and evil-minded men) are fond of bringing forward the argument that colours suffer in grey weather, and that strong sunlight is necessary to all the hues of heaven and earth. Here again there are two words to be said; and it is essential to distinguish. It is true that sun is needed to burnish and bring into bloom the tertiary and dubious colours; the colour of peat, pea-soup, Impressionist sketches, brown velvet coats, olives, grey and blue slates, the complexions of vegetarians, the tints of volcanic rock, chocolate, cocoa, mud, soot, slime, old boots; the delicate shades of these do need the sunlight to bring out the faint beauty that often clings to them. But if you have a healthy negro taste in colour, if you choke your garden with poppies and geraniums, if you paint your house sky-blue and scarlet, if you wear, let us say, a golden top-hat and a crimson frock-coat, you will not only be visible on the greyest day, but you will notice that your costume and environment produce a certain singular effect. You will find, I mean, that rich colours actually look more luminous on a grey day, because they are seen against a sombre background and seem to be burning with a lustre of their own. Against a dark sky all flowers look like fireworks. There is something strange about them, at once vivid and secret, like flowers traced in fire in the phantasmal garden of a witch. A bright blue sky is necessarily the high light of the picture; and its brightness kills all the bright blue flowers. But on a grey day the larkspur looks like fallen heaven; the red daisies are really the red lost eyes of day; and the sunflower is the vice-regent of the sun.

    Lastly, there is this value about the colour that men call colourless; that it suggests in some way the mixed and troubled average of existence, especially in its quality of strife and expectation and promise. Grey is a colour that always seems on the eve of changing to some other colour; of brightening into blue or blanching into white or bursting into green and gold. So we may be perpetually reminded of the indefinite hope that is in doubt itself; and when there is grey weather in our hills or grey hairs in our heads, perhaps they may still remind us of the morning.

The Anarchist

I have now lived for about two months in the country, and have gathered the last rich autumnal fruit of a rural life, which is a strong desire to see London. Artists living in my neighbourhood talk rapturously of the rolling liberty of the landscape, the living peace of woods. But I say to them (with a slight Buckinghamshire accent), "Ah, that is how Cockneys feel. For us real old country people the country is reality; it is the town that is romance. Nature is as plain as one of her pigs, as commonplace, as comic, and as healthy. But civilization is full of poetry, even if it be sometimes an evil poetry. The streets of London are paved with gold; that is, with the very poetry of avarice." With these typically bucolic words I touch my hat and go ambling away on a stick, with a stiffness of gait proper to the Oldest Inhabitant; while in my more animated moments I am taken for the Village Idiot. Exchanging heavy but courteous salutations with other gaffers, I reach the station, where I ask for a ticket for London where the king lives. Such a journey, mingled of provincial fascination and fear, did I successfully perform only a few days ago; and alone and helpless in the capital, found myself in the tangle of roads around the Marble Arch.

A faint prejudice may possess the mind that I have slightly exaggerated my rusticity and remoteness. And yet it is true as I came to that corner of the Park that, for some unreasonable reason of mood, I saw all London as a strange city and the civilization itself as one enormous whim. The Marble Arch itself, in its new insular position, with traffic turning dizzily all about it, struck me as a placid monstrosity. What could be wilder than to have a huge arched gateway, with people going everywhere except under it? If I took down my front door and stood it up all by itself in the middle of my back garden, my village neighbours (in their simplicity) would probably stare. Yet the Marble Arch is now precisely that; an elaborate entrance and the only place by which no one can enter. By the new arrangement its last weak pretence to be a gate has been taken away. The cabman still cannot drive through it, but he can have the delights of riding round it, and even (on foggy nights) the rapture of running into it. It has been raised from the rank of a fiction to the dignity of an obstacle.

As I began to walk across a corner of the Park, this sense of what is strange in cities began to mingle with some sense of what is stern as well as strange. It was one of those queer-coloured winter days when a watery sky changes to pink and grey and green, like an enormous opal. The trees stood up grey and angular, as if in attitudes of agony; and here and there on benches under the trees sat men as grey and angular as they. It was cold even for me, who had eaten a large breakfast and purposed to eat a perfectly Gargantuan lunch; it was colder for the men under the trees. And to eastward through the opalescent haze, the warmer whites and yellows of the houses in Park-lane shone as unsubstantially as if the clouds themselves had taken on the shape of mansions to mock the men who sat there in the cold. But the mansions were real—like the mockery.

No one worth calling a man allows his moods to change his convictions; but it is by moods that we understand other men's convictions. The bigot is not he who knows he is right; every sane man knows he is right. The bigot is he whose emotions and imagination are too cold and weak to feel how it is that other men go wrong. At that moment I felt vividly how men might go wrong, even unto dynamite. If one of those huddled men under the trees had stood up and asked for rivers of blood, it would have been erroneous—but not irrelevant. It would have been appropriate and in the picture; that lurid grey picture of insolence on one side and impotence on the other. It may be true (on the whole it is) that this social machine we have made is better than anarchy. Still, it is a machine; and we have made it. It does hold those poor men helpless: and it does lift those rich men high... and such men—good Lord! By the time I flung myself on a bench beside another man I was half inclined to try anarchy for a change.

The other was of more prosperous appearance than most of the men on such seats; still, he was not what one calls a gentleman, and had probably worked at some time like a human being. He was a small, sharp-faced man, with grave, staring eyes, and a beard somewhat foreign. His clothes were black; respectable and yet casual; those of a man who dressed conventionally because it was a bore to dress unconventionally—as it is. Attracted by this and other things, and wanting an outburst for my bitter social feelings, I tempted him into speech, first about the cold, and then about the General Election. To this the respectable man replied:

"Well, I don't belong to any party myself. I'm an Anarchist."

I looked up and almost expected fire from heaven. This coincidence was like the end of the world. I had sat down feeling that somehow or other Park-lane must be pulled down; and I had sat down beside the man who wanted to pull it down. I bowed in silence for an instant under the approaching apocalypse; and in that instant the man turned sharply and started talking like a torrent.

"Understand me," he said. "Ordinary people think an Anarchist means a man with a bomb in his pocket. Herbert Spencer was an Anarchist. But for that fatal admission of his on page 793, he would be a complete Anarchist. Otherwise, he agrees wholly with Pidge."

This was uttered with such blinding rapidity of syllabification as to be a better test of teetotalism than the Scotch one of saying "Biblical criticism" six times. I attempted to speak, but he began again with the same rippling rapidity.

"You will say that Pidge also admits government in that tenth chapter so easily misunderstood. Bolger has attacked Pidge on those lines. But Bolger has no scientific training. Bolger is a psychometrist, but no sociologist. To any one who has combined a study of Pidge with the earlier and better discoveries of Kruxy, the fallacy is quite clear. Bolger confounds social coercion with coercional social action."

Alarms and Discursions

His rapid rattling mouth shut quite tight suddenly, and he looked steadily and triumphantly at me, with his head on one side. I opened my mouth, and the mere motion seemed to sting him to fresh verbal leaps.

"Yes," he said, "that's all very well. The Finland Group has accepted Bolger. But," he said, suddenly lifting a long finger as if to stop me, "but—Pidge has replied. His pamphlet is published. He has proved that Potential Social Rebuke is not a weapon of the true Anarchist. He has shown that just as religious authority and political authority have gone, so must emotional authority and psychological authority. He has shown—"

I stood up in a sort of daze. "I think you remarked," I said feebly, "that the mere common populace do not quite understand Anarchism"—

"Quite so," he said with burning swiftness; "as I said, they think any Anarchist is a man with a bomb, whereas—"

"But great heavens, man!" I said; "it's the man with the bomb that I understand! I wish you had half his sense. What do I care how many German dons tie themselves in knots about how this society began? My only interest is about how soon it will end. Do you see those fat white houses over in Park-lane, where your masters live?"

He assented and muttered something about concentrations of capital.

"Well," I said, "if the time ever comes when we all storm those houses, will you tell me one thing? Tell me how we shall do it without authority? Tell me how you will have an army of revolt without discipline?"

For the first instant he was doubtful; and I had bidden him farewell, and crossed the street again, when I saw him open his mouth and begin to run after me. He had remembered something out of Pidge.

I escaped, however, and as I leapt on an omnibus I saw again the enormous emblem of the Marble Arch. I saw that massive symbol of the modern mind: a door with no house to it; the gigantic gate of Nowhere.

G. K. Chesterton

How I found the Superman

Readers of Mr. Bernard Shaw and other modern writers may be interested to know that the Superman has been found. I found him; he lives in South Croydon. My success will be a great blow to Mr. Shaw, who has been following quite a false scent, and is now looking for the creature in Blackpool; and as for Mr. Wells's notion of generating him out of gases in a private laboratory, I always thought it doomed to failure. I assure Mr. Wells that the Superman at Croydon was born in the ordinary way, though he himself, of course, is anything but ordinary.

Nor are his parents unworthy of the wonderful being whom they have given to the world. The name of Lady Hypatia Smythe-Browne (now Lady Hypatia Hagg) will never be forgotten in the East End, where she did such splendid social work. Her constant cry of "Save the children!" referred to the cruel neglect of children's eyesight involved in allowing them to play with crudely painted toys. She quoted unanswerable statistics to prove that children allowed to look at violet and vermilion often suffered from failing eyesight in their extreme old age; and it was owing to her ceaseless crusade that the pestilence of the Monkey-on-the-Stick was almost swept from Hoxton. The devoted worker would tramp the streets untiringly, taking away the toys from all the poor children, who were often moved to tears by her kindness. Her good work was interrupted, partly by a new interest in the creed of Zoroaster, and partly by a savage blow from an umbrella. It was inflicted by a dissolute Irish apple-woman, who, on returning from some orgy to her ill-kept apartment, found Lady Hypatia in the bedroom taking down an oleograph, which, to say the least of it, could not really elevate the mind. At this the ignorant and partly intoxicated Celt dealt the social reformer a severe blow, adding to it an absurd accusation of theft. The lady's exquisitely balanced mind received a shock, and it was during a short mental illness that she married Dr. Hagg.

Of Dr. Hagg himself I hope there is no need to speak. Any one even slightly acquainted with those daring experiments in Neo-Individualist Eugenics, which are now the one absorbing interest of the English democracy, must know his name and often commend it to the personal protection of an impersonal power. Early in life he brought to bear that ruthless insight into the history of religions which he had gained in boyhood as an electrical engineer. Later he became one of our greatest geologists; and achieved that bold and bright outlook upon the future of Socialism which only geology can give. At first there seemed something like a rift, a faint, but perceptible, fissure, between his views and those of his aristocratic wife. For she was in favour (to use her own powerful epigram) of protecting the poor against themselves; while he declared pitilessly, in a new and striking metaphor, that the weakest must go to the wall. Eventually, however, the married pair perceived an essential union in the unmistakably modern character of both their views, and in this enlightening and intelligible formula their souls found peace. The result is that this union of the two highest types of our civilization, the fashionable lady and the all but vulgar medical man, has been blessed by the birth of the Superman, that being whom all the labourers in Battersea are so eagerly expecting night and day.

I found the house of Dr. and Lady Hypatia Hagg without much difficulty; it is situated in one of the last straggling streets of Croydon, and overlooked by a line of poplars. I reached the door towards the twilight, and it was natural that I should fancifully see something dark and monstrous in the dim bulk of that house which contained the creature who was more marvellous than the children of men. When I entered the house I was received with exquisite courtesy by Lady Hypatia and her husband; but I found much greater difficulty in actually seeing the Superman, who is now about fifteen years old, and is kept by himself in a quiet room. Even my conversation with the father and mother did not quite clear up the character of this mysterious being. Lady Hypatia, who has a pale and poignant face, and is clad in those impalpable and pathetic greys and greens with which she has brightened so many homes in Hoxton, did not appear to talk of her offspring with any of the vulgar vanity of an ordinary human mother. I took a bold step and asked if the Superman was nice looking.

"He creates his own standard, you see," she replied, with a slight sigh. "Upon that plane he is more than Apollo. Seen from our lower plane, of course—" And she sighed again.

I had a horrible impulse, and said suddenly, "Has he got any hair?"

There was a long and painful silence, and then Dr. Hagg said smoothly: "Everything upon that plane is different; what he has got is not... well, not, of course, what we call hair... but—"

"Don't you think," said his wife, very softly, "don't you think that really, for the sake of argument, when talking to the mere public, one might call it hair?"

"Perhaps you are right," said the doctor after a few moments' reflection. "In connexion with hair like that one must speak in parables."

"Well, what on earth is it," I asked in some irritation, "if it isn't hair? Is it feathers?"

"Not feathers, as we understand feathers," answered Hagg in an awful voice.

I got up in some irritation. "Can I see him, at any rate?" I asked. "I am a journalist, and have no earthly motives except curiosity and personal vanity. I should like to say that I had shaken hands with the Superman."

The husband and wife had both got heavily to their feet, and stood, embarrassed. "Well, of course, you know," said Lady Hypatia, with the really charming smile of the aristocratic hostess. "You know he can't exactly shake hands... not hands, you know.... The structure, of course—"

I broke out of all social bounds, and rushed at the door of the room which I thought to contain the incredible creature. I burst it open; the room was pitch dark. But from in front of me came a small sad yelp, and from behind me a double shriek.

G. K. Chesterton

"You have done it, now!" cried Dr. Hagg, burying his bald brow in his hands. "You have let in a draught on him; and he is dead."

As I walked away from Croydon that night I saw men in black carrying out a coffin that was not of any human shape. The wind wailed above me, whirling the poplars, so that they drooped and nodded like the plumes of some cosmic funeral. "It is, indeed," said Dr. Hagg, "the whole universe weeping over the frustration of its most magnificent birth." But I thought that there was a hoot of laughter in the high wail of the wind.

The New House

Within a stone's throw of my house they are building another house. I am glad they are building it, and I am glad it is within a stone's throw; quite well within it, with a good catapult. Nevertheless, I have not yet cast the first stone at the new house—not being, strictly speaking, guiltless myself in the matter of new houses. And, indeed, in such cases there is a strong protest to be made. The whole curse of the last century has been what is called the Swing of the Pendulum; that is the idea that Man must go alternately from one extreme to the other. It is a shameful and even shocking fancy; it is the denial of the whole dignity of mankind. When Man is alive he stands still. It is only when he is dead that he swings. But whenever one meets modern thinkers (as one often does) progressing towards a madhouse, one always finds, on inquiry, that they have just had a splendid escape from another madhouse. Thus, hundreds of people become Socialists, not because they have tried Socialism and found it nice, but because they have tried Individualism and found it particularly nasty. Thus, many embrace Christian Science solely because they are quite sick of heathen science; they are so tired of believing that everything is matter that they will even take refuge in the revolting fable that everything is mind. Man ought to march somewhere. But modern man (in his sick reaction) is ready to march nowhere—so long as it is the Other End of Nowhere.

The case of building houses is a strong instance of this. Early in the nineteenth century our civilization chose to abandon the Greek and medieval idea of a town, with walls, limited and defined, with a temple for faith and a market-place for politics; and it chose to let the city grow like a jungle with blind cruelty and bestial unconsciousness; so that London and Liverpool are the great cities we now see. Well, people have reacted against that; they have grown tired of living in a city which is as dark and barbaric as a forest only not as beautiful, and there has been an exodus into the country of those who could afford it, and some I could name who can't. Now, as soon as this quite rational recoil occurred, it flew at once to the opposite extreme. People went about with beaming faces, boasting that they were twenty-three miles from a station. Rubbing their hands, they exclaimed in rollicking asides that their butcher only called once a month, and that their baker started out with fresh hot loaves which were quite stale before they reached the table. A man would praise his little house in a quiet valley, but gloomily admit (with a slight shake of the head) that a human habitation on the distant horizon was faintly discernible on a clear day. Rival ruralists would quarrel about which had the most completely inconvenient postal service; and there were many jealous heartburnings if one friend found out any uncomfortable situation which the other friend had thoughtlessly overlooked.

In the feverish summer of this fanaticism there arose the phrase that this or that part of England is being "built over." Now, there is not the slightest objection, in itself, to England being built over by men, any more than there is to its being (as it is already) built over by birds, or by squirrels, or by spiders. But if birds' nests were so thick on a tree that one could see nothing but nests and no leaves at all, I should say that bird civilization was becoming a bit decadent. If whenever I tried to walk down the road I found the whole thoroughfare one crawling carpet of spiders, closely interlocked, I should feel a distress verging on distaste. If one were at every turn crowded, elbowed, overlooked, overcharged, sweated, rack-rented, swindled, and sold up by avaricious and arrogant squirrels, one might at last remonstrate. But the great towns have grown intolerable solely because of such suffocating vulgarities and tyrannies. It is not humanity that disgusts us in the huge cities; it is inhumanity. It is not that there are human beings; but that they are not treated as such. We do not, I hope, dislike men and women; we only dislike their being made into a sort of jam: crushed together so that they are not merely powerless but shapeless. It is not the presence of people that makes London appalling. It is merely the absence of The People.

Therefore, I dance with joy to think that my part of England is being built over, so long as it is being built over in a human way at human intervals and in a human proportion. So long, in short, as I am not myself built over, like a pagan slave buried in the foundations of a temple, or an American clerk in a star-striking pagoda of flats, I am delighted to see the faces and the homes of a race of bipeds, to which I am not only attracted by a strange affection, but to which also (by a touching coincidence) I actually happen to belong. I am not one desiring deserts. I am not Timon of Athens; if my town were Athens I would stay in it. I am not Simeon Stylites; except in the mournful sense that every Saturday I find myself on the top of a newspaper column. I am not in the desert repenting of some monstrous sins; at least, I am repenting of them all right, but not in the desert. I do not want the nearest human house to be too distant to see; that is my objection to the wilderness. But neither do I want the nearest human house to be too close to see; that is my objection to the modern city. I love my fellow-man; I do not want him so far off that I can only observe anything of him through a telescope, nor do I want him so close that I can examine parts of him with a microscope. I want him within a stone's throw of me; so that whenever it is really necessary, I may throw the stone.

Perhaps, after all, it may not be a stone. Perhaps, after all, it may be a bouquet, or a snowball, or a firework, or a Free Trade Loaf; perhaps they will ask for a stone and I shall give them bread. But it is essential that they should be within reach: how can I love my neighbour as myself if he gets out of range for snowballs? There should be no institution out of the reach of an indignant or admiring humanity. I could hit the nearest house quite well with the catapult; but the truth is that the catapult belongs to a little boy I know, and, with characteristic youthful 'selfishness, he has taken it away.

The Wings of Stone

The preceding essay is about a half-built house upon my private horizon; I wrote it sitting in a garden-chair; and as, though it was a week ago, I have scarcely moved since then (to speak of), I do not see why I should not go on writing about it. Strictly speaking, I have moved; I have even walked across a field—a field of turf all fiery in our early summer sunlight—and studied the early angular red skeleton which has turned golden in the sun. It is odd that the skeleton of a house is cheerful when the skeleton of a man is mournful, since we only see it after the man is destroyed. At least, we think the skeleton is mournful; the skeleton himself does not seem to think so. Anyhow, there is something strangely primary and poetic about this sight of the scaffolding and main lines of a human building; it is a pity there is no scaffolding round a human baby. One seems to see domestic life as the daring and ambitious thing that it is, when one looks at those open staircases and empty chambers, those spirals of wind and open halls of sky. Ibsen said that the art of domestic drama was merely to knock one wall out of the four walls of a drawing-room. I find the drawing-room even more impressive when all four walls are knocked out.

I have never understood what people mean by domesticity being tame; it seems to me one of the wildest of adventures. But if you wish to see how high and harsh and fantastic an adventure it is, consider only the actual structure of a house itself. A man may march up in a rather bored way to bed; but at least he is mounting to a height from which he could kill himself. Every rich, silent, padded staircase, with banisters of oak, stair-rods of brass, and busts and settees on every landing, every such staircase is truly only an awful and naked ladder running up into the Infinite to a deadly height. The millionaire who stumps up inside the house is really doing the same thing as the tiler or roof-mender who climbs up outside the house; they are both mounting up into the void. They are both making an escalade of the intense inane. Each is a sort of domestic mountaineer; he is reaching a point from which mere idle falling will kill a man; and life is always worth living while men feel that they may die.

I cannot understand people at present making such a fuss about flying ships and aviation, when men ever since Stonehenge and the Pyramids have done something so much more wild than flying. A grasshopper can go astonishingly high up in the air, his biological limitation and weakness is that he cannot stop there. Hosts of unclean birds and crapulous insects can pass through the sky, but they cannot pass any communication between it and the earth. But the army of man has advanced vertically into infinity, and not been cut off. It can establish outposts in the ether, and yet keep open behind it its erect and insolent road. It would be grand (as in Jules Verne) to fire a cannon-ball at the moon; but would it not be grander to build a railway to the moon? Yet every building of brick or wood is a hint of that high railroad; every chimney points to some star, and every tower is a Tower of Babel. Man rising on these awful and unbroken wings of stone seems to me more majestic and more mystic than man fluttering for an instant on wings of canvas and sticks of steel. How sublime and, indeed, almost dizzy is the thought of these veiled ladders on which we all live, like climbing monkeys! Many a black-coated clerk in a flat may comfort himself for his sombre garb by reflecting that he is like some lonely rook in an immemorial elm. Many a wealthy bachelor on the top floor of a pile of mansions should look forth at morning and try (if possible) to feel like an eagle whose nest just clings to the edge of some awful cliff. How sad that the word "giddy" is used to imply wantonness or levity! It should be a high compliment to a man's exalted spirituality and the imagination to say he is a little giddy.

    I strolled slowly back across the stretch of turf by the sunset, a field of the cloth of gold. As I drew near my own house, its huge size began to horrify me; and when I came to the porch of it I discovered with an incredulity as strong as despair that my house was actually bigger than myself. A minute or two before there might well have seemed to be a monstrous and mythical competition about which of the two should swallow the other. But I was Jonah; my house was the huge and hungry fish; and even as its jaws darkened and closed about me I had again this dreadful fancy touching the dizzy altitude of all the works of man. I climbed the stairs stubbornly, planting each foot with savage care, as if ascending a glacier. When I got to a landing I was wildly relieved, and waved my hat. The very word "landing" has about it the wild sound of some one washed up by the sea. I climbed each flight like a ladder in naked sky. The walls all round me failed and faded into infinity; I went up the ladder to my bedroom as Montrose went up the ladder to the gallows; sic itur ad astro. Do you think this is a little fantastic—even a little fearful and nervous? Believe me, it is only one of the wild and wonderful things that one can learn by stopping at home.

The Three Kinds of Men

Roughly speaking, there are three kinds of people in this world. The first kind of people are People; they are the largest and probably the most valuable class. We owe to this class the chairs we sit down on, the clothes we wear, the houses we live in; and, indeed (when we come to think of it), we probably belong to this class ourselves. The second class may be called for convenience the Poets; they are often a nuisance to their families, but, generally speaking, a blessing to mankind. The third class is that of the Professors or Intellectuals; sometimes described as the thoughtful people; and these are a blight and a desolation both to their families and also to mankind. Of course, the classification sometimes overlaps, like all classification. Some good people are almost poets and some bad poets are almost professors. But the division follows lines of real psychological cleavage. I do not offer it lightly. It has been the fruit of more than eighteen minutes of earnest reflection and research.

The class called People (to which you and I, with no little pride, attach ourselves) has certain casual, yet profound, assumptions, which are called "commonplaces," as that children are charming, or that twilight is sad and sentimental, or that one man fighting three is a fine sight. Now, these feelings are not crude; they are not even simple. The charm of children is very subtle; it is even complex, to the extent of being almost contradictory. It is, at its very plainest, mingled of a regard for hilarity and a regard for helplessness. The sentiment of twilight, in the vulgarest drawing-room song or the coarsest pair of sweethearts, is, so far as it goes, a subtle sentiment. It is strangely balanced between pain and pleasure; it might also be called pleasure tempting pain. The plunge of impatient chivalry by which we all admire a man fighting odds is not at all easy to define separately, it means many things, pity, dramatic surprise, a desire for justice, a delight in experiment and the indeterminate. The ideas of the mob are really very subtle ideas; but the mob does not express them subtly. In fact, it does not express them at all, except on those occasions (now only too rare) when it indulges in insurrection and massacre.

Now, this accounts for the otherwise unreasonable fact of the existence of Poets. Poets are those who share these popular sentiments, but can so express them that they prove themselves the strange and delicate things that they really are. Poets draw out the shy refinement of the rabble. Where the common man covers the queerest emotions by saying, "Rum little kid," Victor Hugo will write "L'art d'etre grand-pere"; where the stockbroker will only say abruptly, "Evenings closing in now," Mr. Yeats will write "Into the twilight"; where the navvy can only mutter something about pluck and being "precious game," Homer will show you the hero in rags in his own hall defying the princes at their banquet. The Poets carry the popular sentiments to a keener and more splendid pitch; but let it always be remembered that it is the popular sentiments that they are carrying. No man ever wrote any good poetry to show that childhood was shocking, or that twilight was gay and farcical, or that a man was contemptible because he had crossed his single sword with three. The people who maintain this are the Professors, or Prigs.

The Poets are those who rise above the people by understanding them. Of course, most of the Poets wrote in prose—Rabelais, for instance, and Dickens. The Prigs rise above the people by refusing to understand them: by saying that all their dim, strange preferences are prejudices and superstitions. The Prigs make the people feel stupid; the Poets make the people feel wiser than they could have imagined that they were. There are many weird elements in this situation. The oddest of all perhaps is the fate of the two factors in practical politics. The Poets who embrace and admire the people are often pelted with stones and crucified. The Prigs who despise the people are often loaded with lands and crowned. In the House of Commons, for instance, there are quite a number of prigs, but comparatively few poets. There are no People there at all.

By poets, as I have said, I do not mean people who write poetry, or indeed people who write anything. I mean such people as, having culture and imagination, use them to understand and share the feelings of their fellows; as against those who use them to rise to what they call a higher plane. Crudely, the poet differs from the mob by his sensibility; the professor differs from the mob by his insensibility. He has not sufficient finesse and sensitiveness to sympathize with the mob. His only notion is coarsely to contradict it, to cut across it, in accordance with some egotistical plan of his own; to tell himself that, whatever the ignorant say, they are probably wrong. He forgets that ignorance often has the exquisite intuitions of innocence.

Let me take one example which may mark out the outline of the contention. Open the nearest comic paper and let your eye rest lovingly upon a joke about a mother-in-law. Now, the joke, as presented for the populace, will probably be a simple joke; the old lady will be tall and stout, the hen-pecked husband will be small and cowering. But for all that, a mother-in-law is not a simple idea. She is a very subtle idea. The problem is not that she is big and arrogant; she is frequently little and quite extraordinarily nice. The problem of the mother-in-law is that she is like the twilight: half one thing and half another. Now, this twilight truth, this fine and even tender embarrassment, might be rendered, as it really is, by a poet, only here the poet would have to be some very penetrating and sincere novelist, like George Meredith, or Mr. H. G. Wells, whose "Ann Veronica" I have just been reading with delight. I would trust the fine poets and novelists because they follow the fairy clue given them in Comic Cuts. But suppose the Professor appears, and suppose he says (as he almost certainly will), "A mother-in-law is merely a fellow-citizen. Considerations of sex should not interfere with comradeship. Regard for age should not influence the intellect. A mother-in-law is merely Another Mind. We should free ourselves from these tribal hierarchies and degrees." Now, when the Professor says this (as he always does), I say to him, "Sir, you are coarser than Comic Cuts. You are more vulgar and blundering than the most elephantine music-hall artiste. You are blinder and grosser than the mob. These vulgar knockabouts have, at least, got hold of a social shade and real mental distinction, though they can only express it clumsily. You are so clumsy that you cannot get hold of it at all. If you really cannot see that the bridegroom's mother and the bride have any reason for constraint or diffidence, then you are neither polite nor humane: you have no sympathy in you for the deep and doubtful hearts of human folk." It is better even to put the difficulty as the vulgar put it than to be pertly unconscious of the difficulty altogether.

The same question might be considered well enough in the old proverb that two is company and three is none. This proverb is the truth put popularly: that is, it is the truth put wrong. Certainly it is untrue that three is no company. Three is splendid company: three is the ideal number for pure comradeship: as in the Three Musketeers. But if you reject the proverb altogether; if you say that two and three are the same sort of company; if you cannot see that there is a wider abyss between two and three than between three and three million—then I regret to inform you that you belong to the Third Class of human beings; that you shall have no company either of two or three, but shall be alone in a howling desert till you die.

G. K. Chesterton

The Steward of the Chiltern Hundreds

The other day on a stray spur of the Chiltern Hills I climbed up upon one of those high, abrupt, windy churchyards from which the dead seem to look down upon all the living. It was a mountain of ghosts as Olympus was a mountain of gods. In that church lay the bones of great Puritan lords, of a time when most of the power of England was Puritan, even of the Established Church. And below these uplifted bones lay the huge and hollow valleys of the English countryside, where the motors went by every now and then like meteors, where stood out in white squares and oblongs in the chequered forest many of the country seats even of those same families now dulled with wealth or decayed with Toryism. And looking over that deep green prospect on that luminous yellow evening, a lovely and austere thought came into my mind, a thought as beautiful as the green wood and as grave as the tombs. The thought was this: that I should like to go into Parliament, quarrel with my party, accept the Stewardship of the Chiltern Hundreds, and then refuse to give it up.

We are so proud in England of our crazy constitutional anomalies that I fancy that very few readers indeed will need to be told about the Steward of the Chiltern Hundreds. But in case there should be here or there one happy man who has never heard of such twisted tomfooleries, I will rapidly remind you what this legal fiction is. As it is quite a voluntary, sometimes even an eager, affair to get into Parliament, you would naturally suppose that it would be also a voluntary matter to get out again. You would think your fellow-members would be indifferent, or even relieved to see you go; especially as (by another exercise of the shrewd, illogical old English common sense) they have carefully built the room too small for the people who have to sit in it. But not so, my pippins, as it says in the "Iliad." If you are merely a member of Parliament (Lord knows why) you can't resign. But if you are a Minister of the Crown (Lord knows why) you can. It is necessary to get into the Ministry in order to get out of the House; and they have to give you some office that doesn't exist or that nobody else wants and thus unlock the door. So you go to the Prime Minister, concealing your air of fatigue, and say, "It has been the ambition of my life to be Steward of the Chiltern Hundreds." The Prime Minister then replies, "I can imagine no man more fitted both morally and mentally for that high office." He then gives it you, and you hurriedly leave, reflecting how the republics of the Continent reel anarchically to and fro for lack of a little solid English directness and simplicity.

Now, the thought that struck me like a thunderbolt as I sat on the Chiltern slope was that I would like to get the Prime Minister to give me the Chiltern Hundreds, and then startle and disturb him by showing the utmost interest in my work. I should profess a general knowledge of my duties, but wish to be instructed in the details. I should ask to see the Under-Steward and the Under-Under-Steward, and all the fine staff of experienced permanent officials who are the glory of this department. And, indeed, my enthusiasm would not be wholly unreal. For as far as I can recollect the original duties of a Steward of the Chiltern Hundreds were to put down the outlaws and brigands in that part of the world. Well, there are a great many outlaws and brigands in that part of the world still, and though their methods have so largely altered as to require a corresponding alteration in the tactics of the Steward, I do not see why an energetic and public-spirited Steward should not nab them yet.

For the robbers have not vanished from the old high forests to the west of the great city. The thieves have not vanished; they have grown so large that they are invisible. You do not see the word "Asia" written across a map of that neighbourhood; nor do you see the word "Thief" written across the countrysides of England; though it is really written in equally large letters. I know men governing despotically great stretches of that country, whose every step in life has been such that a slip would have sent them to Dartmoor; but they trod along the high hard wall between right and wrong, the wall as sharp as a swordedge, as softly and craftily and lightly as a cat. The vastness of their silent violence itself obscured what they were at; if they seem to stand for the rights of property it is really because they have so often invaded them. And if they do not break the laws, it is only because they make them.

But after all we only need a Steward of the Chiltern Hundreds who really understands cats and thieves. Men hunt one animal differently from another; and the rich could catch swindlers as dexterously as they catch otters or antlered deer if they were really at all keen upon doing it. But then they never have an uncle with antlers; nor a personal friend who is an otter. When some of the great lords that lie in the churchyard behind me went out against their foes in those deep woods beneath I wager that they had bows against the bows of the outlaws, and spears against the spears of the robber knights. They knew what they were about; they fought the evildoers of their age with the weapons of their age. If the same common sense were applied to commercial law, in forty-eight hours it would be all over with the American Trusts and the African forward finance. But it will not be done: for the governing class either does not care, or cares very much, for the criminals, and as for me, I had a delusive opportunity of being Constable of Beaconsfield (with grossly inadequate powers), but I fear I shall never really be Steward of the Chiltern Hundreds.

G. K. Chesterton

The Field of Blood

In my daily paper this morning I read the following interesting paragraphs, which take my mind back to an England which I do not remember and which, therefore (perhaps), I admire.

"Nearly sixty years ago—on 4 September, 1850—the Austrian General Haynau, who had gained an unenviable fame throughout the world by his ferocious methods in suppressing the Hungarian revolution in 1849, while on a visit to this country, was belaboured in the streets of London by the draymen of Messrs. Barclay, Perkins and Co., whose brewery he had just inspected in company of an adjutant. Popular delight was so great that the Government of the time did not dare to prosecute the assailants, and the General—the 'women-flogger,' as he was called by the people—had to leave these shores without remedy.

"He returned to his own country and settled upon his estate at Szekeres, which is close to the commune above-mentioned. By his will the estate passed to his daughter, after whose death it was to be presented to the commune. This daughter has just died, but the Communal Council, after much deliberation, has declined to accept the gift, and ordered that the estate should be left to fall out of cultivation, and be called the 'Bloody Meadow.'"

Now that is an example of how things happen under an honest democratical impulse. I do not dwell specially on the earlier part of the story, though the earlier part of the story is astonishingly interesting. It recalls the days when Englishmen were potential lighters; that is, potential rebels. It is not for lack of agonies of intellectual anger: the Sultan and the late King Leopold have been denounced as heartily as General Haynau. But I doubt if they would have been physically thrashed in the London streets.

It is not the tyrants that are lacking, but the draymen. Nevertheless, it is not upon the historic heroes of Barclay, Perkins and Co. that I build all my hope. Fine as it was, it was not a full and perfect revolution. A brewer's drayman beating an eminent European General with a stick, though a singularly bright and pleasing vision, is not a complete one. Only when the brewer's drayman beats the brewer with a stick shall we see the clear and radiant sunrise of British self-government. The fun will really start when we begin to thump the oppressors of England as well as the oppressors of Hungary. It is, however, a definite decline in the spiritual character of draymen that now they can thump neither one nor the other.

But, as I have already suggested, my real quarrel is not about the first part of the extract, but about the second. Whether or no the draymen of Barclay and Perkins have degenerated, the Commune which includes Szekeres has not degenerated. By the way, the Commune which includes Szekeres is called Kissekeres; I trust that this frank avowal will excuse me from the necessity of mentioning either of these places again by name. The

Alarms and Discursions

Commune is still capable of performing direct democratic actions, if necessary, with a stick.

I say with a stick, not with sticks, for that is the whole argument about democracy. A people is a soul; and if you want to know what a soul is, I can only answer that it is something that can sin and that can sacrifice itself. A people can commit theft; a people can confess theft; a people can repent of theft. That is the idea of the republic. Now, most modern people have got into their heads the idea that democracies are dull, drifting things, a mere black swarm or slide of clerks to their accustomed doom. In most modern novels and essays it is insisted (by way of contrast) that a walking gentleman may have ad-ventures as he walks. It is insisted that an aristocrat can commit crimes, because an aristocrat always cultivates liberty. But, in truth, a people can have adventures, as Israel did crawling through the desert to the promised land. A people can do heroic deeds; a people can commit crimes; the French people did both in the Revolution; the Irish people have done both in their much purer and more honourable progress.

But the real answer to this aristocratic argument which seeks to identify democracy with a drab utilitarianism may be found in action such as that of the Hungarian Commune—whose name I decline to repeat. This Commune did just one of those acts that prove that a separate people has a separate personality; it threw something away. A man can throw a bank note into the fire. A man can fling a sack of corn into the river. The bank-note may be burnt as a satisfaction of some scruple; the corn may be destroyed as a sacrifice to some god. But whenever there is sacrifice we know there is a single will. Men may be disputatious and doubtful, may divide by very narrow majorities in their debate about how to gain wealth. But men have to be uncommonly unanimous in order to refuse wealth. It wants a very complete committee to burn a bank note in the office grate. It needs a highly religious tribe really to throw corn into the river. This self-denial is the test and definition of self-government.

I wish I could feel certain that any English County Council or Parish Council would be single enough to make that strong gesture of a romantic refusal; could say, "No rents shall be raised from this spot; no grain shall grow in this spot; no good shall come of this spot; it shall remain sterile for a sign." But I am afraid they might answer, like the eminent sociologist in the story, that it was "wiste of spice."

G. K. Chesterton

The Strangeness of Luxury

It is an English misfortune that what is called "public spirit" is so often a very private spirit; the legitimate but strictly individual ideals of this or that person who happens to have the power to carry them out. When these private principles are held by very rich people, the result is often the blackest and most repulsive kind of despotism, which is benevolent despotism. Obviously it is the public which ought to have public spirit. But in this country and at this epoch this is exactly what it has not got. We shall have a public washhouse and a public kitchen long before we have a public spirit; in fact, if we had a public spirit we might very probably do without the other things. But if England were properly and naturally governed by the English, one of the first results would probably be this: that our standard of excess or defect in property would be changed from that of the plutocrat to that of the moderately needy man. That is, that while property might be strictly respected, everything that is necessary to a clerk would be felt and considered on quite a different plane from anything which is a very great luxury to a clerk. This sane distinction of sentiment is not instinctive at present, because our standard of life is that of the governing class, which is eternally turning luxuries into necessities as fast as pork is turned into sausages; and which cannot remember the beginning of its needs and cannot get to the end of its novelties.

Take, for the sake of argument, the case of the motor. Doubtless the duke now feels it as necessary to have a motor as to have a roof, and in a little while he may feel it equally necessary to have a flying ship. But this does not prove (as the reactionary sceptics always argue) that a motor really is just as necessary as a roof. It only proves that a man can get used to an artificial life: it does not prove that there is no natural life for him to get used to. In the broad bird's-eye view of common sense there abides a huge disproportion between the need for a roof and the need for an aeroplane; and no rush of inventions can ever alter it. The only difference is that things are now judged by the abnormal needs, when they might be judged merely by the normal needs. The best aristocrat sees the situation from an aeroplane. The good citizen, in his loftiest moments, goes no further than seeing it from the roof.

It is not true that luxury is merely relative. It is not true that it is only an expensive novelty which we may afterwards come to think a necessity. Luxury has a firm philosophical meaning; and where there is a real public spirit luxury is generally allowed for, sometimes rebuked, but always recognized instantly. To the healthy soul there is something in the very nature of certain pleasures which warns us that they are exceptions, and that if they become rules they will become very tyrannical rules.

Take a harassed seamstress out of the Harrow Road and give her one lightning hour in a motorcar, and she will probably feel it as splendid, but strange, rare, and even terrible. But this is not (as the relativists say) merely because she has never been in a car before. She has never been in the middle of a Somerset cowslip meadow before; but if you put her there she does not think it terrifying or extraordinary, but merely pleasant and free and a little lonely. She does not think the motor monstrous because it is new. She thinks it monstrous because she has eyes in her head; she thinks it monstrous because it is monstrous. That is, her mothers and grandmothers, and the whole race by whose life she lives, have had, as a matter of fact, a roughly recognizable mode of living; sitting in a green field was a part of it; travelling as quick as a cannon ball was not. And we should not look down on the seamstress because she mechanically emits a short sharp scream whenever the motor begins to move. On the contrary, we ought to look up to the seamstress, and regard her cry as a kind of mystic omen or revelation of nature, as the old Goths used to consider the howls emitted by chance females when annoyed. For that ritual yell is really a mark of moral health—of swift response to the stimulations and changes of life. The seamstress is wiser than all the learned ladies, precisely because she can still feel that a motor is a different sort of thing from a meadow. By the accident of her economic imprisonment it is even possible that she may have seen more of the former than the latter. But this has not shaken her cyclopean sagacity as to which is the natural thing and which the artificial. If not for her, at least for humanity as a whole, there is little doubt about which is the more normally attainable. It is considerably cheaper to sit in a meadow and see motors go by than to sit in a motor and see meadows go by.

To me personally, at least, it would never seem needful to own a motor, any more than to own an avalanche. An avalanche, if you have luck, I am told, is a very swift, successful, and thrilling way of coming down a hill. It is distinctly more stirring, say, than a glacier, which moves an inch in a hundred years. But I do not divide these pleasures either by excitement or convenience, but by the nature of the thing itself. It seems human to have a horse or bicycle, because it seems human to potter about; and men cannot work horses, nor can bicycles work men, enormously far afield of their ordinary haunts and affairs.

But about motoring there is something magical, like going to the moon; and I say the thing should be kept exceptional and felt as something breathless and bizarre. My ideal hero would own his horse, but would have the moral courage to hire his motor. Fairy tales are the only sound guidebooks to life; I like the Fairy Prince to ride on a white pony out of his father's stables, which are of ivory and gold. But if in the course of his adventures he finds it necessary to travel on a flaming dragon, I think he ought to give the dragon back to the witch at the end of the story. It is a mistake to have dragons about the place.

For there is truly an air of something weird about luxury; and it is by this that healthy human nature has always smelt and suspected it. All romances that deal in extreme luxury, from the "Arabian Nights" to the novels of Ouida and Disraeli, have, it may be noted, a singular air of dream and occasionally of nightmare. In such imaginative debauches there is something as occasional as intoxication; if that is still counted occasional.

G. K. Chesterton

Life in those preposterous palaces would be an agony of dullness; it is clear we are meant to visit them only as in a flying vision. And what is true of the old freaks of wealth, flavour and fierce colour and smell, I would say also of the new freak of wealth, which is speed. I should say to the duke, when I entered his house at the head of an armed mob, "I do not object to your having exceptional pleasures, if you have them exceptionally. I do not mind your enjoying the strange and alien energies of science, if you feel them strange and alien, and not your own. But in condemning you (under the Seventeenth Section of the Eighth Decree of the Republic) to hire a motor-car twice a year at Margate, I am not the enemy of your luxuries, but, rather, the protector of them."

That is what I should say to the duke. As to what the duke would say to me, that is another matter, and may well be deferred.

The Triumph of the Donkey

Doubtless the unsympathetic might state my doctrine that one should not own a motor like a horse, but rather use it like a flying dragon in the simpler form that I will always go motoring in somebody else's car. My favourite modern philosopher (Mr. W. W. Jacobs) describes a similar case of spiritual delicacy misunderstood. I have not the book at hand, but I think that Job Brown was reproaching Bill Chambers for wasteful drunkenness, and Henery Walker spoke up for Bill, and said he scarcely ever had a glass but what somebody else paid for it, and there was "unpleasantness all round then."

Being less sensitive than Bill Chambers (or whoever it was) I will risk this rude perversion of my meaning, and concede that I was in a motor-car yesterday, and the motor-car most certainly was not my own, and the journey, though it contained nothing that is specially unusual on such journeys, had running through it a strain of the grotesque which was at once wholesome and humiliating. The symbol of that influence was that ancient symbol of the humble and humorous—a donkey.

When first I saw the donkey I saw him in the sunlight as the unearthly gargoyle that he is. My friend had met me in his car (I repeat firmly, in his car) at the little painted station in the middle of the warm wet woods and hop-fields of that western country. He proposed to drive me first to his house beyond the village before starting for a longer spin of adventure, and we rattled through those rich green lanes which have in them something singularly analogous to fairy tales: whether the lanes produced the fairies or (as I believe) the fairies produced the lanes. All around in the glimmering hop-yards stood those little hop-kilns like stunted and slanting spires. They look like dwarfish churches—in fact, rather like many modern churches I could mention, churches all of them small and each of them a little crooked. In this elfin atmosphere we swung round a sharp corner and half-way up a steep, white hill, and saw what looked at first like a tall, black monster against the sun. It appeared to be a dark and dreadful woman walking on wheels and waving long ears like a bat's. A second glance told me that she was not the local witch in a state of transition; she was only one of the million tricks of perspective. She stood up in a small wheeled cart drawn by a donkey; the donkey's ears were just set behind her head, and the whole was black against the light.

Perspective is really the comic element in everything. It has a pompous Latin name, but it is incurably Gothic and grotesque. One simple proof of this is that it is always left out of all dignified and decorative art. There is no perspective in the Elgin Marbles, and even the essentially angular angels in mediaeval stained glass almost always (as it says in "Patience") contrive to look both angular and flat. There is something intrinsically disproportionate and outrageous in the idea of the distant objects dwindling and growing dwarfish, the closer objects swelling enormous and intolerable. There is something frantic in the notion that

G. K. Chesterton

one's own father by walking a little way can be changed by a blast of magic to a pigmy. There is something farcical in the fancy that Nature keeps one's uncle in an infinite number of sizes, according to where he is to stand. All soldiers in retreat turn into tin soldiers; all bears in rout into toy bears; as if on the ultimate horizon of the world everything was sardonically doomed to stand up laughable and little against heaven.

It was for this reason that the old woman and her donkey struck us first when seen from behind as one black grotesque. I afterwards had the chance of seeing the old woman, the cart, and the donkey fairly, in flank and in all their length. I saw the old woman and the donkey PASSANT, as they might have appeared heraldically on the shield of some heroic family. I saw the old woman and the donkey dignified, decorative, and flat, as they might have marched across the Elgin Marbles. Seen thus under an equal light, there was nothing specially ugly about them; the cart was long and sufficiently comfortable; the donkey was stolid and sufficiently respectable; the old woman was lean but sufficiently strong, and even smiling in a sour, rustic manner. But seen from behind they looked like one black monstrous animal; the dark donkey cars seemed like dreadful wings, and the tall dark back of the woman, erect like a tree, seemed to grow taller and taller until one could almost scream.

Then we went by her with a blasting roar like a railway train, and fled far from her over the brow of the hill to my friend's home.

There we paused only for my friend to stock the car with some kind of picnic paraphernalia, and so started again, as it happened, by the way we had come. Thus it fell that we went shattering down that short, sharp hill again before the poor old woman and her donkey had managed to crawl to the top of it; and seeing them under a different light, I saw them very differently. Black against the sun, they had seemed comic; but bright against greenwood and grey cloud, they were not comic but tragic; for there are not a few things that seem fantastic in the twilight, and in the sunlight are sad. I saw that she had a grand, gaunt mask of ancient honour and endurance, and wide eyes sharpened to two shining points, as if looking for that small hope on the horizon of human life. I also saw that her cart contained carrots.

"Don't you feel, broadly speaking, a beast," I asked my friend, "when you go so easily and so fast?" For we had crashed by so that the crazy cart must have thrilled in every stick of it.

My friend was a good man, and said, "Yes. But I don't think it would do her any good if I went slower."

"No," I assented after reflection. "Perhaps the only pleasure we can give to her or any one else is to get out of their sight very soon."

My friend availed himself of this advice in no niggard spirit; I felt as if we were fleeing for our lives in throttling fear after some frightful atrocity. In truth, there is only one difference left between the secrecy of the two social classes: the poor hide themselves in darkness and the rich hide themselves in distance. They both hide.

Alarms and Discursions

As we shot like a lost boat over a cataract down into a whirlpool of white roads far below, I saw afar a black dot crawling like an insect. I looked again: I could hardly believe it. There was the slow old woman, with her slow old donkey, still toiling along the main road. I asked my friend to slacken, but when he said of the car, "She's wanting to go," I knew it was all up with him. For when you have called a thing female you have yielded to it utterly. We passed the old woman with a shock that must have shaken the earth: if her head did not reel and her heart quail, I know not what they were made of. And when we had fled perilously on in the gathering dark, spurning hamlets behind us, I suddenly called out, "Why, what asses we are! Why, it's She that is brave—she and the donkey. We are safe enough; we are artillery and plate-armour: and she stands up to us with matchwood and a snail! If you had grown old in a quiet valley, and people began firing cannon-balls as big as cabs at you in your seventieth year, wouldn't you jump—and she never moved an eyelid. Oh! we go very fast and very far, no doubt—"

As I spoke came a curious noise, and my friend, instead of going fast, began to go very slow; then he stopped; then he got out. Then he said, "And I left the Stepney behind."

The grey moths came out of the wood and the yellow stars came out to crown it, as my friend, with the lucidity of despair, explained to me (on the soundest scientific principles, of course) that nothing would be any good at all. We must sleep the night in the lane, except in the very unlikely event of some one coming by to carry a message to some town. Twice I thought I heard some tiny sound of such approach, and it died away like wind in the trees, and the motorist was already asleep when I heard it renewed and realized. Something certainly was approaching. I ran up the road—and there it was. Yes, It—and She. Thrice had she come, once comic and once tragic and once heroic. And when she came again it was as if in pardon on a pure errand of prosaic pity and relief. I am quite serious. I do not want you to laugh. It is not the first time a donkey has been received seriously, nor one riding a donkey with respect.

G. K. Chesterton

The Wheel

In a quiet and rustic though fairly famous church in my neighbourhood there is a window supposed to represent an Angel on a Bicycle. It does definitely and indisputably represent a nude youth sitting on a wheel; but there is enough complication in the wheel and sanctity (I suppose) in the youth to warrant this working description. It is a thing of florid Renascence outline, and belongs to the highly pagan period which introduced all sorts of objects into ornament: personally I can believe in the bicycle more than in the angel. Men, they say, are now imitating angels; in their flying-machines, that is: not in any other respect that I have heard of. So perhaps the angel on the bicycle (if he is an angel and if it is a bicycle) was avenging himself by imitating man. If so, he showed that high order of intellect which is attributed to angels in the mediaeval books, though not always (perhaps) in the mediaeval pictures.

For wheels are the mark of a man quite as much as wings are the mark of an angel. Wheels are the things that are as old as mankind and yet are strictly peculiar to man, that are prehistoric but not pre-human.

A distinguished psychologist, who is well acquainted with physiology, has told me that parts of himself are certainly levers, while other parts are probably pulleys, but that after feeling himself carefully all over, he cannot find a wheel anywhere. The wheel, as a mode of movement, is a purely human thing. On the ancient escutcheon of Adam (which, like much of the rest of his costume, has not yet been discovered) the heraldic emblem was a wheel—passant. As a mode of progress, I say, it is unique. Many modern philosophers, like my friend before mentioned, are ready to find links between man and beast, and to show that man has been in all things the blind slave of his mother earth. Some, of a very different kind, are even eager to show it; especially if it can be twisted to the discredit of religion. But even the most eager scientists have often admitted in my hearing that they would be surprised if some kind of cow approached them moving solemnly on four wheels. Wings, fins, flappers, claws, hoofs, webs, trotters, with all these the fantastic families of the earth come against us and close around us, fluttering and flapping and rustling and galloping and lumbering and thundering; but there is no sound of wheels.

I remember dimly, if, indeed, I remember aright, that in some of those dark prophetic pages of Scripture, that seem of cloudy purple and dusky gold, there is a passage in which the seer beholds a violent dream of wheels. Perhaps this was indeed the symbolic declaration of the spiritual supremacy of man. Whatever the birds may do above or the fishes beneath his ship, man is the only thing to steer; the only thing to be conceived as steering. He may make the birds his friends, if he can. He may make the fishes his gods, if he chooses. But most certainly he will not believe a bird at the masthead; and it is hardly likely that he will even permit a fish at the helm. He is, as Swinburne says, helmsman and chief: he is literally the Man at the Wheel.

The wheel is an animal that is always standing on its head; only "it does it so rapidly that no philosopher has ever found out which is its head." Or if the phrase be felt as more exact, it is an animal that is always turning head over heels and progressing by this principle. Some fish, I think, turn head over heels (supposing them, for the sake of argument, to have heels); I have a dog who nearly did it; and I did it once myself when I was very small. It was an accident, and, as delightful novelist, Mr. De Morgan, would say, it never can happen again. Since then no one has accused me of being upside down except mentally: and I rather think that there is something to be said for that; especially as typified by the rotary symbol. A wheel is the sublime paradox; one part of it is always going forward and the other part always going back. Now this, as it happens, is highly similar to the proper condition of any human soul or any political state. Every sane soul or state looks at once backwards and forwards; and even goes backwards to come on.

For those interested in revolt (as I am) I only say meekly that one cannot have a Revolution without revolving. The wheel, being a logical thing, has reference to what is behind as well as what is before. It has (as every society should have) a part that perpetually leaps helplessly at the sky and a part that perpetually bows down its head into the dust. Why should people be so scornful of us who stand on our heads? Bowing down one's head in the dust is a very good thing, the humble beginning of all happiness. When we have bowed our heads in the dust for a little time the happiness comes; and then (leaving our heads' in the humble and reverent position) we kick up our heels behind in the air. That is the true origin of standing on one's head; and the ultimate defence of paradox. The wheel humbles itself to be exalted; only it does it a little quicker than I do.

G. K. Chesterton

Five Hundred and Fifty-five

Life is full of a ceaseless shower of small coincidences: too small to be worth mentioning except for a special purpose, often too trifling even to be noticed, any more than we notice one snowflake falling on another. It is this that lends a frightful plausibility to all false doctrines and evil fads. There are always such crowds of accidental arguments for anything. If I said suddenly that historical truth is generally told by red-haired men, I have no doubt that ten minutes' reflection (in which I decline to indulge) would provide me with a handsome list of instances in support of it. I remember a riotous argument about Bacon and Shakespeare in which I offered quite at random to show that Lord Rosebery had written the works of Mr. W. B. Yeats. No sooner had I said the words than a torrent of coincidences rushed upon my mind. I pointed out, for instance, that Mr. Yeats's chief work was "The Secret Rose." This may easily be paraphrased as "The Quiet or Modest Rose"; and so, of course, as the Primrose. A second after I saw the same suggestion in the combination of "rose" and "bury." If I had pursued the matter, who knows but I might have been a raving maniac by this time.

We trip over these trivial repetitions and exactitudes at every turn, only they are too trivial even for conversation. A man named Williams did walk into a strange house and murder a man named Williamson; it sounds like a sort of infanticide. A journalist of my acquaintance did move quite unconsciously from a place called Overstrand to a place called Overroads. When he had made this escape he was very properly pursued by a voting card from Battersea, on which a political agent named Burn asked him to vote for a political candidate named Burns. And when he did so another coincidence happened to him: rather a spiritual than a material coincidence; a mystical thing, a matter of a magic number.

For a sufficient number of reasons, the man I know went up to vote in Battersea in a drifting and even dubious frame of mind. As the train slid through swampy woods and sullen skies there came into his empty mind those idle and yet awful questions which come when the mind is empty. Fools make cosmic systems out of them; knaves make profane poems out of them; men try to crush them like an ugly lust. Religion is only the responsible reinforcement of common courage and common sense. Religion only sets up the normal mood of health against the hundred moods of disease.

But there is this about such ghastly empty enigmas, that they always have an answer to the obvious answer, the reply offered by daily reason. Suppose a man's children have gone swimming; suppose he is suddenly throttled by the senseless—fear that they are drowned. The obvious answer is, "Only one man in a thousand has his children drowned." But a deeper voice (deeper, being as deep as hell) answers, "And why should not you—be the thousandth man?" What is true of tragic doubt is true also of trivial doubt. The voter's guardian devil said to him, "If you don't vote to-day you can do fifteen things which will quite certainly do some good somewhere, please a friend, please a child, please a maddened publisher. And what good do you expect to do by voting? You don't think your man will get in by one vote, do you?" To this he knew the answer of common sense, "But if everybody said that, nobody would get in at all." And then there came that deeper voice from Hades, "But you are not settling what everybody shall do, but what one person on one occasion shall do. If this afternoon you went your way about more solid things, how would it matter and who would ever know?" Yet somehow the voter drove on blindly through the blackening London roads, and found somewhere a tedious polling station and recorded his tiny vote.

    The politician for whom the voter had voted got in by five hundred and fifty-five votes. The voter read this next morning at breakfast, being in a more cheery and expansive mood, and found something very fascinating not merely in the fact of the majority, but even in the form of it. There was something symbolic about the three exact figures; one felt it might be a sort of motto or cipher. In the great book of seals and cloudy symbols there is just such a thundering repetition. Six hundred and sixty-six was the Mark of the Beast. Five hundred and fifty-five is the Mark of the Man; the triumphant tribune and citizen. A number so symmetrical as that really rises out of the region of science into the region of art. It is a pattern, like the egg-and-dart ornament or the Greek key. One might edge a wall-paper or fringe a robe with a recurring decimal. And while the voter luxuriated in this light exactitude of the numbers, a thought crossed his mind and he almost leapt to his feet. "Why, good heavens!" he cried. "I won that election; and it was won by one vote! But for me it would have been the despicable, broken-backed, disjointed, inharmonious figure five hundred and fifty-four. The whole artistic point would have vanished. The Mark of the Man would have disappeared from history. It was I who with a masterful hand seized the chisel and carved the hieroglyph—complete and perfect. I clutched the trembling hand of Destiny when it was about to make a dull square four and forced it to make a nice curly five. Why, but for me the Cosmos would have lost a coincidence!" After this outburst the voter sat down and finished his breakfast.

G. K. Chesterton

Ethandune

Perhaps you do not know where Ethandune is. Nor do I; nor does anybody. That is where the somewhat sombre fun begins. I cannot even tell you for certain whether it is the name of a forest or a town or a hill. I can only say that in any case it is of the kind that floats and is unfixed. If it is a forest, it is one of those forests that march with a million legs, like the walking trees that were the doom of Macbeth. If it is a town, it is one of those towns that vanish, like a city of tents. If it is a hill, it is a flying hill, like the mountain to which faith lends wings. Over a vast dim region of England this dark name of Ethandune floats like an eagle doubtful where to swoop and strike, and, indeed, there were birds of prey enough over Ethandune, wherever it was. But now Ethandune itself has grown as dark and drifting as the black drifts of the birds.

And yet without this word that you cannot fit with a meaning and hardly with a memory, you would be sitting in a very different chair at this moment and looking at a very different tablecloth. As a practical modern phrase I do not commend it; if my private critics and correspondents in whom I delight should happen to address me "G. K. Chesterton, Poste Restante, Ethandune," I fear their letters would not come to hand. If two hurried commercial travellers should agree to discuss a business matter at Ethandune from 5 to 5.15, I am afraid they would grow old in the district as white-haired wanderers. To put it plainly, Ethandune is anywhere and nowhere in the western hills; it is an English mirage. And yet but for this doubtful thing you would have probably no Daily News on Saturday and certainly no church on Sunday. I do not say that either of these two things is a benefit; but I do say that they are customs, and that you would not possess them except through this mystery. You would not have Christmas puddings, nor (probably) any puddings; you would not have Easter eggs, probably not poached eggs, I strongly suspect not scrambled eggs, and the best historians are decidedly doubtful about curried eggs. To cut a long story short (the longest of all stories), you would not have any civilization, far less any Christian civilization. And if in some moment of gentle curiosity you wish to know why you are the polished sparkling, rounded, and wholly satisfactory citizen which you obviously are, then I can give you no more definite answer geographical or historical; but only toll in your ears the tone of the uncaptured name—Ethandune.

I will try to state quite sensibly why it is as important as it is. And yet even that is not easy. If I were to state the mere fact from the history books, numbers of people would think it equally trivial and remote, like some war of the Picts and Scots. The points perhaps might be put in this way. There is a certain spirit in the world which breaks everything off short. There may be magnificence in the smashing; but the thing is smashed. There may be a certain splendour; but the splendour is sterile: it abolishes all future splendours. I mean (to take a working example), York Minster covered with flames might happen to be quite as beautiful as York Minster covered with carvings. But the carvings produce more carvings. The flames produce nothing but a little black heap. When any act has this cul-de-sac quality it matters little whether it is done by a book or a sword, by a clumsy battle-axe or a chemical bomb. The case is the same with ideas. The pessimist may be a proud figure when he curses all the stars; the optimist may be an even prouder figure when he blesses them all. But the real test is not in the energy, but in the effect. When the optimist has said, "All things are interesting," we are left free; we can be interested as much or as little as we please. But when the pessimist says, "No things are interesting," it may be a very witty remark: but it is the last witty remark that can be made on the subject. He has burnt his cathedral; he has had his blaze and the rest is ashes. The sceptics, like bees, give their one sting and die. The pessimist must be wrong, because he says the last word.

Now, this spirit that denies and that destroys had at one period of history a dreadful epoch of military superiority. They did burn York Minster, or at least, places of the same kind. Roughly speaking, from the seventh century to the tenth, a dense tide of darkness, of chaos and brainless cruelty, poured on these islands and on the western coasts of the Continent, which well-nigh cut them off from all the white man's culture for ever. And this is the final human test; that the varied chiefs of that vague age were remembered or forgotten according to how they had resisted this almost cosmic raid. Nobody thought of the modern nonsense about races; everybody thought of the human race and its highest achievements. Arthur was a Celt, and may have been a fabulous Celt; but he was a fable on the right side. Charlemagne may have been a Gaul or a Goth, but he was not a barbarian; he fought for the tradition against the barbarians, the nihilists. And for this reason also, for this reason, in the last resort, only, we call the saddest and in some ways the least successful of the Wessex kings by the title of Alfred the Great. Alfred was defeated by the barbarians again and again, he defeated the barbarians again and again; but his victories were almost as vain as his defeats. Fortunately he did not believe in the Time Spirit or the Trend of Things or any such modern rubbish, and therefore kept pegging away. But while his failures and his fruitless successes have names still in use (such as Wilton, Basing, and Ashdown), that last epic battle which really broke the barbarian has remained without a modern place or name. Except that it was near Chippenham, where the Danes gave up their swords and were baptized, no one can pick out certainly the place where you and I were saved from being savages for ever.

But the other day under a wild sunset and moonrise I passed the place which is best reputed as Ethandune, a high, grim upland, partly bare and partly shaggy; like that savage and sacred spot in those great imaginative lines about the demon lover and the waning moon. The darkness, the red wreck of sunset, the yellow and lurid moon, the long fantastic shadows, actually created that sense of monstrous incident which is the dramatic side of landscape. The bare grey slopes seemed to rush downhill like routed hosts; the dark clouds drove across like riven banners; and the moon was like a golden dragon, like the Golden Dragon of Wessex.

As we crossed a tilt of the torn heath I saw suddenly between myself and the moon a black shapeless pile higher than a house. The atmosphere was so intense that I really thought of a pile of dead Danes, with some phantom conqueror on the top of it. Fortunately I was crossing these wastes with a friend who knew more history than I; and he told me that this was a barrow older than Alfred, older than the Romans, older perhaps than the Britons; and no man knew whether it was a wall or a trophy or a tomb. Ethandune is still a drifting name; but it gave me a queer emotion to think that, sword in hand, as the Danes poured with the torrents of their blood down to Chippenham, the great king may have lifted up his head and looked at that oppressive shape, suggestive of something and yet suggestive of nothing; may have looked at it as we did, and understood it as little as we.

The Flat Freak

Some time ago a Sub-Tropical Dinner was given by some South African millionaire. I forget his name; and so, very likely, does he. The humour of this was so subtle and haunting that it has been imitated by another millionaire, who has given a North Pole Dinner in a grand hotel, on which he managed to spend gigantic sums of money. I do not know how he did it; perhaps they had silver for snow and great sapphires for lumps of ice. Anyhow, it seems to have cost rather more to bring the Pole to London than to take Peary to the Pole. All this, one would say, does not concern us. We do not want to go to the Pole—or to the hotel. I, for one, cannot imagine which would be the more dreary and disgusting—the real North Pole or the sham one. But as a mere matter of psychology (that merry pastime) there is a question that is not unentertaining.

Why is it that all this scheme of ice and snow leaves us cold? Why is it that you and I feel that we would (on the whole) rather spend the evening with two or three stable boys in a pot-house than take part in that pallid and Arctic joke? Why does the modern millionaire's jest—bore a man to death with the mere thought of it? That it does bore a man to death I take for granted, and shall do so until somebody writes to me in cold ink and tells me that he really thinks it funny.

Now, it is not a sufficient explanation to say that the joke is silly. All jokes are silly; that is what they are for. If you ask some sincere and elemental person, a woman, for instance, what she thinks of a good sentence from Dickens, she will say that it is "too silly." When Mr. Weller, senior, assured Mr. Weller, junior, that "circumvented" was "a more tenderer word" than "circumscribed," the remark was at least as silly as it was sublime. It is vain, then, to object to "senseless jokes." The very definition of a joke is that it need have no sense; except that one wild and supernatural sense which we call the sense of humour. Humour is meant, in a literal sense, to make game of man; that is, to dethrone him from his official dignity and hunt him like game. It is meant to remind us human beings that we have things about us as ungainly and ludicrous as the nose of the elephant or the neck of the giraffe. If laughter does not touch a sort of fundamental folly, it does not do its duty in bringing us back to an enormous and original simplicity. Nothing has been worse than the modern notion that a clever man can make a joke without taking part in it; without sharing in the general absurdity that such a situation creates. It is unpardonable conceit not to laugh at your own jokes. Joking is undignified; that is why it is so good for one's soul. Do not fancy you can be a detached wit and avoid being a buffoon; you cannot. If you are the Court Jester you must be the Court Fool.

Whatever it is, therefore, that wearies us in these wealthy jokes (like the North Pole Dinner) it is not merely that men make fools of themselves. When Dickens described Mr. Chuckster, Dickens was, strictly speaking, making a fool of himself; for he was making a fool out of himself. And every kind of real lark, from acting a charade to making a pun, does consist in restraining one's nine hundred and ninety-nine serious selves and letting the fool loose. The dullness of the millionaire joke is much deeper. It is not silly at all; it is solely stupid. It does not consist of ingenuity limited, but merely of inanity expanded. There is considerable difference between a wit making a fool of himself and a fool making a wit of himself.

The true explanation, I fancy, may be stated thus. We can all remember it in the case of the really inspiriting parties and fooleries of our youth. The only real fun is to have limited materials and a good idea. This explains the perennial popularity of impromptu private theatricals. These fascinate because they give such a scope for invention and variety with the most domestic restriction of machinery. A tea-cosy may have to do for an Admiral's cocked hat; it all depends on whether the amateur actor can swear like an Admiral. A hearth-rug may have to do for a bear's fur; it all depends on whether the wearer is a polished and versatile man of the world and can grunt like a bear. A clergyman's hat (to my own private and certain knowledge) can be punched and thumped into the exact shape of a policeman's helmet; it all depends on the clergyman. I mean it depends on his permission; his imprimatur; his nihil obstat. Clergymen can be policemen; rugs can rage like wild animals; tea-cosies can smell of the sea; if only there is at the back of them all one bright and amusing idea. What is really funny about Christmas charades in any average home is that there is a contrast between commonplace resources and one comic idea. What is deadly dull about the millionaire-banquets is that there is a contrast between colossal resources and no idea.

That is the abyss of inanity in such feasts—it may be literally called a yawning abyss. The abyss is the vast chasm between the money power employed and the thing it is employed on. To make a big joke out of a broomstick, a barrow and an old hat—that is great. But to make a small joke out of mountains of emeralds and tons of gold—surely that is humiliating! The North Pole is not a very good joke to start with. An icicle hanging on one's nose is a simple sort of humour in any case. If a set of spontaneous mummers got the effect cleverly with cut crystals from the early Victorian chandelier there might really be something suddenly funny in it. But what should we say of hanging diamonds on a hundred human noses merely to make that precious joke about icicles?

What can be more abject than the union of elaborate and recherche arrangements with an old and obvious point? The clown with the red-hot poker and the string of sausages is all very well in his way. But think of a string of pate de foie gras sausages at a guinea a piece! Think of a red-hot poker cut out of a single ruby! Imagine such fantasticalities of expense with such a tameness and staleness of design.

We may even admit the practical joke if it is domestic and simple. We may concede that apple-pie beds and butter-slides are sometimes useful things for the education of pompous persons living the Higher Life. But imagine a man making a butter-slide and telling everybody it was made with the most expensive butter. Picture an apple-pie bed of purple and cloth of gold. It is not hard to see that such schemes would lead simultaneously to a double boredom; weariness of the costly and complex method and of the meagre and trivial thought. This is the true analysis, I think of that chill of tedium that strikes to the soul of any intelligent man when he hears of such elephantine pranks. That is why we feel that Freak Dinners would not even be freakish. That is why we feel that expensive Arctic feasts would probably be a frost.

If it be said that such things do no harm, I hasten, in one sense, at least, to agree. Far from it; they do good. They do good in the most vital matter of modern times; for they prove and print in huge letters the truth which our society must learn or perish. They prove that wealth in society as now constituted does not tend to get into the hands of the thrifty or the capable, but actually tends to get into the hands of wastrels and imbeciles. And it proves that the wealthy class of to-day is quite as ignorant about how to enjoy itself as about how to rule other people. That it cannot make its government govern or its education educate we may take as a trifling weakness of oligarchy; but pleasure we do look to see in such a class; and it has surely come to its decrepitude when it cannot make its pleasures please.

G. K. Chesterton

The Garden of the Sea

One sometimes hears from persons of the chillier type of culture the remark that plain country people do not appreciate the beauty of the country. This is an error rooted in the intellectual pride of mediocrity; and is one of the many examples of a truth in the idea that extremes meet. Thus, to appreciate the virtues of the mob one must either be on a level with it (as I am) or be really high up, like the saints. It is roughly the same with aesthetics; slang and rude dialect can be relished by a really literary taste, but not by a merely bookish taste. And when these cultivated cranks say that rustics do not talk of Nature in an appreciative way, they really mean that they do not talk in a bookish way. They do not talk bookishly about clouds or stones, or pigs or slugs, or horses or anything you please. They talk piggishly about pigs; and sluggishly, I suppose, about slugs; and are refreshingly horsy about horses. They speak in a stony way of stones; they speak in a cloudy way of clouds; and this is surely the right way. And if by any chance a simple intelligent person from the country comes in contact with any aspect of Nature unfamiliar and arresting, such a person's comment is always worth remark. It is sometimes an epigram, and at worst it is never a quotation.

Consider, for instance, what wastes of wordy imitation and ambiguity the ordinary educated person in the big towns could pour out on the subject of the sea. A country girl I know in the county of Buckingham had never seen the sea in her life until the other day. When she was asked what she thought of it she said it was like cauliflowers. Now that is a piece of pure literature—vivid, entirely independent and original, and perfectly true. I had always been haunted with an analogous kinship which I could never locate; cabbages always remind me of the sea and the sea always reminds me of cabbages. It is partly, perhaps, the veined mingling of violet and green, as in the sea a purple that is almost dark red may mix with a green that is almost yellow, and still be the blue sea as a whole. But it is more the grand curves of the cabbage that curl over cavernously like waves, and it is partly again that dreamy repetition, as of a pattern, that made two great poets, Eschylus and Shakespeare, use a word like "multitudinous" of the ocean. But just where my fancy halted the Buckinghamshire young woman rushed (so to speak) to my imaginative rescue. Cauliflowers are twenty times better than cabbages, for they show the wave breaking as well as curling, and the efflorescence of the branching foam, blind bubbling, and opaque. Moreover, the strong lines of life are suggested; the arches of the rushing waves have all the rigid energy of green stalks, as if the whole sea were one great green plant with one immense white flower rooted in the abyss.

Now, a large number of delicate and superior persons would refuse to see the force in that kitchen garden comparison, because it is not connected with any of the ordinary maritime sentiments as stated in books and songs. The aesthetic amateur would say that he knew what large and philosophical thoughts he ought to have by the boundless deep. He would say that he was not a greengrocer who would think first of greens. To which I should reply, like Hamlet, apropos of a parallel profession, "I would you were so honest a man." The mention of "Hamlet" reminds me, by the way, that besides the girl who had never seen the sea, I knew a girl who had never seen a stage-play. She was taken to "Hamlet," and she said it was very sad. There is another case of going to the primordial point which is overlaid by learning and secondary impressions. We are so used to thinking of "Hamlet" as a problem that we sometimes quite forget that it is a tragedy, just as we are so used to thinking of the sea as vast and vague, that we scarcely notice when it is white and green.

 But there is another quarrel involved in which the young gentleman of culture comes into violent collision with the young lady of the cauliflowers. The first essential of the merely bookish view of the sea is that it is boundless, and gives a sentiment of infinity. Now it is quite certain, I think, that the cauliflower simile was partly created by exactly the opposite impression, the impression of boundary and of barrier. The girl thought of it as a field of vegetables, even as a yard of vegetables. The girl was right. The ocean only suggests infinity when you cannot see it; a sea mist may seem endless, but not a sea. So far from being vague and vanishing, the sea is the one hard straight line in Nature. It is the one plain limit; the only thing that God has made that really looks like a wall. Compared to the sea, not only sun and cloud are chaotic and doubtful, but solid mountains and standing forests may be said to melt and fade and flee in the presence of that lonely iron line. The old naval phrase, that the seas are England's bulwarks, is not a frigid and artificial metaphor; it came into the head of some genuine sea-dog, when he was genuinely looking at the sea. For the edge of the sea is like the edge of a sword; it is sharp, military, and decisive; it really looks like a bolt or bar, and not like a mere expansion. It hangs in heaven, grey, or green, or blue, changing in colour, but changeless in form, behind all the slippery contours of the land and all the savage softness of the forests, like the scales of God held even. It hangs, a perpetual reminder of that divine reason and justice which abides behind all compromises and all legitimate variety; the one straight line; the limit of the intellect; the dark and ultimate dogma of the world.

G. K. Chesterton

The Sentimentalist

"Sentimentalism is the most broken reed on which righteousness can lean"; these were, I think, the exact words of a distinguished American visitor at the Guildhall, and may Heaven forgive me if I do him a wrong. It was spoken in illustration of the folly of supporting Egyptian and other Oriental nationalism, and it has tempted me to some reflections on the first word of the sentence.

The Sentimentalist, roughly speaking, is the man who wants to eat his cake and have it. He has no sense of honour about ideas; he will not see that one must pay for an idea as for anything else. He will not see that any worthy idea, like any honest woman, can only be won on its own terms, and with its logical chain of loyalty. One idea attracts him; another idea really inspires him; a third idea flatters him; a fourth idea pays him. He will have them all at once in one wild intellectual harem, no matter how much they quarrel and contradict each other. The Sentimentalist is a philosophic profligate, who tries to capture every mental beauty without reference to its rival beauties; who will not even be off with the old love before he is on with the new. Thus if a man were to say, "I love this woman, but I may some day find my affinity in some other woman," he would be a Sentimentalist. He would be saying, "I will eat my wedding-cake and keep it." Or if a man should say, "I am a Republican, believing in the equality of citizens; but when the Government has given me my peerage I can do infinite good as a kind landlord and a wise legislator"; then that man would be a Sentimentalist. He would be trying to keep at the same time the classic austerity of equality and also the vulgar excitement of an aristocrat. Or if a man should say, "I am in favour of religious equality; but I must preserve the Protestant Succession," he would be a Sentimentalist of a grosser and more improbable kind.

This is the essence of the Sentimentalist: that he seeks to enjoy every idea without its sequence, and every pleasure without its consequence.

Now it would really be hard to find a worse case of this inconsequent sentimentalism than the theory of the British Empire advanced by Mr. Roosevelt himself in his attack on Sentimentalists. For the Imperial theory, the Roosevelt and Kipling theory, of our relation to Eastern races is simply one of eating the Oriental cake (I suppose a Sultana Cake) and at the same time leaving it alone.

Now there are two sane attitudes of a European statesman towards Eastern peoples, and there are only two.

First, he may simply say that the less we have to do with them the better; that whether they are lower than us or higher they are so catastrophically different that the more we go our way and they go theirs the better for all parties concerned. I will confess to some tenderness for this view. There is much to be said for letting that calm immemorial life of slave and sultan, temple and palm tree flow on as it has always flowed. The best reason of all, the reason that affects me most finally, is that if we left the rest of the world alone we might have some time for attending to our own affairs, which are urgent to the point of excruciation. All history points to this; that intensive cultivation in the long run triumphs over the widest extensive cultivation; or, in other words, that making one's own field superior is far more effective than reducing other people's fields to inferiority. If you cultivate your own garden and grow a specially large cabbage, people will probably come to see it. Whereas the life of one selling small cabbages round the whole district is often forlorn.

Now, the Imperial Pioneer is essentially a commercial traveller; and a commercial traveller is essentially a person who goes to see people because they don't want to see him. As long as empires go about urging their ideas on others, I always have a notion that the ideas are no good. If they were really so splendid, they would make the country preaching them a wonder of the world. That is the true ideal; a great nation ought not to be a hammer, but a magnet. Men went to the mediaeval Sorbonne because it was worth going to. Men went to old Japan because only there could they find the unique and exquisite old Japanese art. Nobody will ever go to modern Japan (nobody worth bothering about, I mean), because modern Japan has made the huge mistake of going to the other people: becoming a common empire. The mountain has condescended to Mahomet; and henceforth Mahomet will whistle for it when he wants it.

That is my political theory: that we should make England worth copying instead of telling everybody to copy her.

But it is not the only possible theory. There is another view of our relations to such places as Egypt and India which is entirely tenable. It may be said, "We Europeans are the heirs of the Roman Empire; when all is said we have the largest freedom, the most exact science, the most solid romance. We have a deep though undefined obligation to give as we have received from God; because the tribes of men are truly thirsting for these things as water. All men really want clear laws: we can give clear laws. All men really want hygiene: we can give hygiene. We are not merely imposing Western ideas. We are simply fulfilling human ideas—for the first time."

On this line, I think, it is possible to justify the forts of Africa and the railroads of Asia; but on this line we must go much further. If it is our duty to give our best, there can be no doubt about what is our best. The greatest thing our Europe has made is the Citizen: the idea of the average man, free and full of honour, voluntarily invoking on his own sin the just vengeance of his city. All else we have done is mere machinery for that: railways exist only to carry the Citizen; forts only to defend him; electricity only to light him, medicine only to heal him. Popularism, the idea of the people alive and patiently feeding history, that we cannot give; for it exists everywhere, East and West. But democracy, the idea of the people fighting and governing—that is the only thing we have to give.

Those are the two roads. But between them weakly wavers the Sentimentalist—that is, the Imperialist of the Roosevelt school. He wants to have it both ways, to have the splendours of success without the perils.

G. K. Chesterton

Europe may enslave Asia, because it is flattering: but Europe must not free Asia, because that is responsible. It tickles his Imperial taste that Hindoos should have European hats: it is too dangerous if they have European heads. He cannot leave Asia Asiatic: yet he dare not contemplate Asia as European. Therefore he proposes to have in Egypt railway signals, but not flags; despatch boxes, but not ballot boxes.

In short, the Sentimentalist decides to spread the body of Europe without the soul.

The White Horses

It is within my experience, which is very brief and occasional in this matter, that it is not really at all easy to talk in a motor-car. This is fortunate; first, because, as a whole, it prevents me from motoring; and second because, at any given moment, it prevents me from talking. The difficulty is not wholly due to the physical conditions, though these are distinctly unconversational. FitzGerald's Omar, being a pessimist, was probably rich, and being a lazy fellow, was almost certainly a motorist. If any doubt could exist on the point, it is enough to say that, in speaking of the foolish profits, Omar has defined the difficulties of colloquial motoring with a precision which cannot be accidental. "Their words to wind are scattered; and their mouths are stopped with dust." From this follows not (as many of the cut-and-dried philosophers would say) a savage silence and mutual hostility, but rather one of those rich silences that make the mass and bulk of all friendship; the silence of men rowing the same boat or fighting in the same battle-line.

It happened that the other day I hired a motor-car, because I wanted to visit in very rapid succession the battle-places and hiding-places of Alfred the Great; and for a thing of this sort a motor is really appropriate. It is not by any means the best way of seeing the beauty of the country; you see beauty better by walking, and best of all by sitting still. But it is a good method in any enterprise that involves a parody of the military or governmental quality—anything which needs to know quickly the whole contour of a county or the rough, relative position of men and towns. On such a journey, like jagged lightning, I sat from morning till night by the side of the chauffeur; and we scarcely exchanged a word to the hour. But by the time the yellow stars came out in the villages and the white stars in the skies, I think I understood his character; and I fear he understood mine.

He was a Cheshire man with a sour, patient, and humorous face; he was modest, though a north countryman, and genial, though an expert. He spoke (when he spoke at all) with a strong northland accent; and he evidently was new to the beautiful south country, as was clear both from his approval and his complaints. But though he came from the north he was agricultural and not commercial in origin; he looked at the land rather than the towns, even if he looked at it with a somewhat more sharp and utilitarian eye. His first remark for some hours was uttered when we were crossing the more coarse and desolate heights of Salisbury Plain. He remarked that he had always thought that Salisbury Plain was a plain. This alone showed that he was new to the vicinity. But he also said, with a critical frown, "A lot of this land ought to be good land enough. Why don't they use it?" He was then silent for some more hours.

At an abrupt angle of the slopes that lead down from what is called (with no little humour) Salisbury Plain, I saw suddenly, as by accident, something I was looking for—that is, something I did not expect to see. We are all supposed to be trying to walk into heaven; but we should be uncommonly astonished if we suddenly walked into it. As I was leaving Salisbury Plain (to put it roughly) I lifted up my eyes and saw the White Horse of Britain.

One or two truly fine poets of the Tory and Protestant type, such as Swinburne and Mr. Rudyard Kipling, have eulogized England under the image of white horses, meaning the white-maned breakers of the Channel. This is right and natural enough. The true philosophical Tory goes back to ancient things because he thinks they will be anarchic things. It would startle him very much to be told that there are white horses of artifice in England that may be older than those wild white horses of the elements. Yet it is truly so. Nobody knows how old are those strange green and white hieroglyphics, those straggling quadrupeds of chalk, that stand out on the sides of so many of the Southern Downs. They are possibly older than Saxon and older than Roman times. They may well be older than British, older than any recorded times. They may go back, for all we know, to the first faint seeds of human life on this planet. Men may have picked a horse out of the grass long before they scratched a horse on a vase or pot, or messed and massed any horse out of clay. This may be the oldest human art—before building or graving. And if so, it may have first happened in another geological age, before the sea burst through the narrow Straits of Dover. The White Horse may have begun in Berkshire when there were no white horses at Folkestone or Newhaven. That rude but evident white outline that I saw across the valley may have been begun when Britain was not an island. We forget that there are many places where art is older than nature.

We took a long detour through somewhat easier roads, till we came to a breach or chasm in the valley, from which we saw our friend the White Horse once more. At least, we thought it was our friend the White Horse; but after a little inquiry we discovered to our astonishment that it was another friend and another horse. Along the leaning flanks of the same fair valley there was (it seemed) another white horse; as rude and as clean, as ancient and as modern, as the first. This, at least, I thought must be the aboriginal White Horse of Alfred, which I had always heard associated with his name. And yet before we had driven into Wantage and seen King Alfred's quaint grey statue in the sun, we had seen yet a third white horse. And the third white horse was so hopelessly unlike a horse that we were sure that it was genuine. The final and original white horse, the white horse of the White Horse Vale, has that big, babyish quality that truly belongs to our remotest ancestors. It really has the prehistoric, preposterous quality of Zulu or New Zealand native drawings. This at least was surely made by our fathers when they were barely men; long before they were civilized men.

But why was it made? Why did barbarians take so much trouble to make a horse nearly as big as a hamlet; a horse who could bear no hunter, who could drag no load? What was this titanic, sub-conscious instinct for spoiling a beautiful green slope with a very ugly white quadruped? What (for the matter of that) is this whole hazardous fancy of humanity ruling the earth, which may have begun with white horses, which may by no means end with twenty horse-power cars? As I rolled away out of that country, I was still cloudily considering how ordinary men ever came to want to make such strange chalk horses, when my chauffeur startled me by speaking for the first time for nearly two hours. He suddenly let go one of the handles and pointed at a gross green bulk of down that happened to swell above us. "That would be a good place," he said.

Naturally I referred to his last speech of some hours before; and supposed he meant that it would be promising for agriculture. As a fact, it was quite unpromising; and this made me suddenly understand the quiet ardour in his eye. All of a sudden I saw what he really meant. He really meant that this would be a splendid place to pick out another white horse. He knew no more than I did why it was done; but he was in some unthinkable prehistoric tradition, because he wanted to do it. He became so acute in sensibility that he could not bear to pass any broad breezy hill of grass on which there was not a white horse. He could hardly keep his hands off the hills. He could hardly leave any of the living grass alone.

Then I left off wondering why the primitive man made so many white horses. I left off troubling in what sense the ordinary eternal man had sought to scar or deface the hills. I was content to know that he did want it; for I had seen him wanting it.

G. K. Chesterton

The Long Bow

I find myself still sitting in front of the last book by Mr. H. G. Wells, I say stunned with admiration, my family says sleepy with fatigue. I still feel vaguely all the things in Mr. Wells's book which I agree with; and I still feel vividly the one thing that I deny. I deny that biology can destroy the sense of truth, which alone can even desire biology. No truth which I find can deny that I am seeking the truth. My mind cannot find anything which denies my mind... But what is all this? This is no sort of talk for a genial essay. Let us change the subject; let us have a romance or a fable or a fairy tale.

Come, let us tell each other stories. There was once a king who was very fond of listening to stories, like the king in the Arabian Nights. The only difference was that, unlike that cynical Oriental, this king believed all the stories that he heard. It is hardly necessary to add that he lived in England. His face had not the swarthy secrecy of the tyrant of the thousand tales; on the contrary, his eyes were as big and innocent as two blue moons; and when his yellow beard turned totally white he seemed to be growing younger. Above him hung still his heavy sword and horn, to remind men that he had been a tall hunter and warrior in his time: indeed, with that rusted sword he had wrecked armies. But he was one of those who will never know the world, even when they conquer it. Besides his love of this old Chaucerian pastime of the telling of tales, he was, like many old English kings, specially interested in the art of the bow. He gathered round him great archers of the stature of Ulysses and Robin Hood, and to four of these he gave the whole government of his kingdom. They did not mind governing his kingdom; but they were sometimes a little bored with the necessity of telling him stories. None of their stories were true; but the king believed all of them, and this became very depressing. They created the most preposterous romances; and could not get the credit of creating them. Their true ambition was sent empty away. They were praised as archers; but they desired to be praised as poets. They were trusted as men, but they would rather have been admired as literary men.

At last, in an hour of desperation, they formed themselves into a club or conspiracy with the object of inventing some story which even the king could not swallow. They called it The League of the Long Bow; thus attaching themselves by a double bond to their motherland of England, which has been steadily celebrated since the Norman Conquest for its heroic archery and for the extraordinary credulity of its people.

At last it seemed to the four archers that their hour had come. The king commonly sat in a green curtained chamber, which opened by four doors, and was surmounted by four turrets. Summoning his champions to him on an April evening, he sent out each of them by a separate door, telling him to return at morning with the tale of his journey. Every champion bowed low, and, girding on great armour as for awful adventures, retired to some part of the garden to think of a lie. They did not want to think of a lie which would deceive the king; any lie would do that. They wanted to think of a lie so outrageous that it would not deceive him, and that was a serious matter.

The first archer who returned was a dark, quiet, clever fellow, very dexterous in small matters of mechanics. He was more interested in the science of the bow than in the sport of it. Also he would only shoot at a mark, for he thought it cruel to kill beasts and birds, and atrocious to kill men. When he left the king he had gone out into the wood and tried all sorts of tiresome experiments about the bending of branches and the impact of arrows; when even he found it tiresome he returned to the house of the four turrets and narrated his adventure. "Well," said the king, "what have you been shooting?" "Arrows," answered the archer. "So I suppose," said the king smiling; "but I mean, I mean what wild things have you shot?" "I have shot nothing but arrows," answered the bowman obstinately. "When I went out on to the plain I saw in a crescent the black army of the Tartars, the terrible archers whose bows are of bended steel, and their bolts as big as javelins. They spied me afar off, and the shower of their arrows shut out the sun and made a rattling roof above me. You know, I think it wrong to kill a bird, or worm, or even a Tartar. But such is the precision and rapidity of perfect science that, with my own arrows, I split every arrow as it came against me. I struck every flying shaft as if it were a flying bird. Therefore, Sire, I may say truly, that I shot nothing but arrows." The king said, "I know how clever you engineers are with your fingers." The archer said, "Oh," and went out.

The second archer, who had curly hair and was pale, poetical, and rather effeminate, had merely gone out into the garden and stared at the moon. When the moon had become too wide, blank, and watery, even for his own wide, blank, and watery eyes, he came in again. And when the king said "What have you been shooting?" he answered with great volubility, "I have shot a man; not a man from Tartary, not a man from Europe, Asia, Africa, or America; not a man on this earth at all. I have shot the Man in the Moon." "Shot the Man in the Moon?" repeated the king with something like a mild surprise. "It is easy to prove it," said the archer with hysterical haste. "Examine the moon through this particularly powerful telescope, and you will no longer find any traces of a man there." The king glued his big blue idiotic eye to the telescope for about ten minutes, and then said, "You are right: as you have often pointed out, scientific truth can only be tested by the senses. I believe you." And the second archer went out, and being of a more emotional temperament burst into tears.

The third archer was a savage, brooding sort of man with tangled hair and dreamy eyes, and he came in without any preface, saying, "I have lost all my arrows. They have turned into birds." Then as he saw that they all stared at him, he said "Well, you know everything changes on the earth; mud turns into marigolds, eggs turn into chickens; one can even breed dogs into quite different shapes. Well, I shot my arrows at the awful eagles that clash their wings round the Himalayas; great golden eagles as big as elephants, which snap the tall trees by perching on them. My arrows fled so far over mountain and valley that they turned slowly into fowls in their flight. See here," and he threw down a dead bird and laid an arrow beside it. "Can't you see they are the same structure. The straight shaft is the backbone; the sharp point is the beak; the feather is the rudimentary plumage. It is merely modification and evolution." After a silence the king nodded gravely and said, "Yes; of course everything is evolution." At this the third archer suddenly and violently left the room, and was heard in some distant part of the building making extraordinary noises either of sorrow or of mirth.

The fourth archer was a stunted man with a face as dead as wood, but with wicked little eyes close together, and very much alive. His comrades dissuaded him from going in because they said that they had soared up into the seventh heaven of living lies, and that there was literally nothing which the old man would not believe. The face of the little archer became a little more wooden as he forced his way in, and when he was inside he looked round with blinking bewilderment. "Ha, the last," said the king heartily, "welcome back again!" There was a long pause, and then the stunted archer said, "What do you mean by 'again'? I have never been here before." The king stared for a few seconds, and said, "I sent you out from this room with the four doors last night." After another pause the little man slowly shook his head. "I never saw you before," he said simply; "you never sent me out from anywhere. I only saw your four turrets in the distance, and strayed in here by accident. I was born in an island in the Greek Archipelago; I am by profession an auctioneer, and my name is Punk." The king sat on his throne for seven long instants like a statue; and then there awoke in his mild and ancient eyes an awful thing; the complete conviction of untruth. Every one has felt it who has found a child obstinately false. He rose to his height and took down the heavy sword above him, plucked it out naked, and then spoke. "I will believe your mad tales about the exact machinery of arrows; for that is science. I will believe your mad tales about traces of life in the moon; for that is science. I will believe your mad tales about jellyfish turning into gentlemen, and everything turning into anything; for that is science. But I will not believe you when you tell me what I know to be untrue. I will not believe you when you say that you did not all set forth under my authority and out of my house. The other three may conceivably have told the truth; but this last man has certainly lied. Therefore I will kill him." And with that the old and gentle king ran at the man with uplifted sword; but he was arrested by the roar of happy laughter, which told the world that there is, after all, something which an Englishman will not swallow.

The Modern Scrooge

Mr. Vernon-Smith, of Trinity, and the Social Settlement, Tooting, author of "A Higher London" and "The Boyg System at Work," came to the conclusion, after looking through his select and even severe library, that Dickens's "Christmas Carol" was a very suitable thing to be read to charwomen. Had they been men they would have been forcibly subjected to Browning's "Christmas Eve" with exposition, but chivalry spared the charwomen, and Dickens was funny, and could do no harm. His fellow worker Wimpole would read things like "Three Men in a Boat" to the poor; but Vernon-Smith regarded this as a sacrifice of principle, or (what was the same thing to him) of dignity. He would not encourage them in their vulgarity; they should have nothing from him that was not literature. Still Dickens was literature after all; not literature of a high order, of course, not thoughtful or purposeful literature, but literature quite fitted for charwomen on Christmas Eve.

He did not, however, let them absorb Dickens without due antidotes of warning and criticism. He explained that Dickens was not a writer of the first rank, since he lacked the high seriousness of Matthew Arnold. He also feared that they would find the characters of Dickens terribly exaggerated. But they did not, possibly because they were meeting them every day. For among the poor there are still exaggerated characters; they do not go to the Universities to be universified. He told the charwomen, with progressive brightness, that a mad wicked old miser like Scrooge would be really quite impossible now; but as each of the charwomen had an uncle or a grandfather or a father-in-law who was exactly like Scrooge, his cheerfulness was not shared. Indeed, the lecture as a whole lacked something of his firm and elastic touch, and towards the end he found himself rambling, and in a sort of abstraction, talking to them as if they were his fellows. He caught himself saying quite mystically that a spiritual plane (by which he meant his plane) always looked to those on the sensual or Dickens plane, not merely austere, but desolate. He said, quoting Bernard Shaw, that we could all go to heaven just as we can all go to a classical concert, but if we did it would bore us. Realizing that he was taking his flock far out of their depth, he ended somewhat hurriedly, and was soon receiving that generous applause which is a part of the profound ceremonialism of the working classes. As he made his way to the door three people stopped him, and he answered them heartily enough, but with an air of hurry which he would not have dreamed of showing to people of his own class. One was a little schoolmistress who told him with a sort of feverish meekness that she was troubled because an Ethical Lecturer had said that Dickens was not really Progressive; but she thought he was Progressive; and surely he was Progressive. Of what being Progressive was she had no more notion than a whale. The second person implored him for a subscription to some soup kitchen or cheap meal; and his refined features sharpened; for this, like literature, was a matter of principle with him.

"Quite the wrong method," he said, shaking his head and pushing past. "Nothing any good but the Boyg system." The third stranger, who was male, caught him on the step as he came out into the snow and starlight; and asked him point blank for money. It was a part of Vernon-Smith's principles that all such persons are prosperous impostors; and like a true mystic he held to his principles in defiance of his five senses, which told him that the night was freezing and the man very thin and weak. "If you come to the Settlement between four and five on Friday week," he said, "inquiries will be made." The man stepped back into the snow with a not ungraceful gesture as of apology; he had frosty silver hair, and his lean face, though in shadow, seemed to wear something like a smile. As Vernon-Smith stepped briskly into the street, the man stooped down as if to do up his bootlace. He was, however, guiltless of any such dandyism; and as the young philanthropist stood pulling on his gloves with some particularity, a heavy snowball was suddenly smashed into his face. He was blind for a black instant; then as some of the snow fell, saw faintly, as in a dim mirror of ice or dreamy crystal, the lean man bowing with the elegance of a dancing master, and saying amiably, "A Christmas box." When he had quite cleared his face of snow the man had vanished.

For three burning minutes Cyril Vernon-Smith was nearer to the people and more their brother than he had been in his whole high-stepping pedantic existence; for if he did not love a poor man, he hated one. And you never really regard a labourer as your equal until you can quarrel with him. "Dirty cad!" he muttered. "Filthy fool! Mucking with snow like a beastly baby! When will they be civilized? Why, the very state of the street is a disgrace and a temptation to such tomfools. Why isn't all this snow cleared away and the street made decent?"

To the eye of efficiency, there was, indeed, something to complain of in the condition of the road. Snow was banked up on both sides in white walls and towards the other and darker end of the street even rose into a chaos of low colourless hills. By the time he reached them he was nearly knee deep, and was in a far from philanthropic frame of mind. The solitude of the little streets was as strange as their white obstruction, and before he had ploughed his way much further he was convinced that he had taken a wrong turning, and fallen upon some formless suburb unvisited before. There was no light in any of the low, dark houses; no light in anything but the blank emphatic snow. He was modern and morbid; hellish isolation hit and held him suddenly; anything human would have relieved the strain, if it had been only the leap of a garotter. Then the tender human touch came indeed; for another snowball struck him, and made a star on his back. He turned with fierce joy, and ran after a boy escaping; ran with dizzy and violent speed, he knew not for how long. He wanted the boy; he did not know whether he loved or hated him. He wanted humanity; he did not know whether he loved or hated it.

As he ran he realized that the landscape around him was changing in shape though not in colour. The houses seemed to dwindle and disappear in hills of snow as if buried; the snow seemed to rise in tattered outlines of crag and cliff and crest, but he thought nothing of all these impossibilities until the boy turned to bay. When he did he saw the child was queerly beautiful, with gold red hair, and a face as serious as complete happiness. And when he spoke to the boy his own question surprised him, for he said for the first time in his life, "What am I doing here?" And the little boy, with very grave eyes, answered, "I suppose you are dead."

He had (also for the first time) a doubt of his spiritual destiny. He looked round on a towering landscape of frozen peaks and plains, and said, "Is this hell?" And as the child stared, but did not answer, he knew it was heaven.

All over that colossal country, white as the world round the Pole, little boys were playing, rolling each other down dreadful slopes, crushing each other under falling cliffs; for heaven is a place where one can fight for ever without hurting. Smith suddenly remembered how happy he had been as a child, rolling about on the safe sandhills around Conway.

Right above Smith's head, higher than the cross of St. Paul's, but curving over him like the hanging blossom of a harebell, was a cavernous crag of snow. A hundred feet below him, like a landscape seen from a balloon, lay snowy flats as white and as far away. He saw a little boy stagger, with many catastrophic slides, to that toppling peak; and seizing another little boy by the leg, send him flying away down to the distant silver plains. There he sank and vanished in the snow as if in the sea; but coming up again like a diver rushed madly up the steep once more, rolling before him a great gathering snowball, gigantic at last, which he hurled back at the mountain crest, and brought both the boy and the mountain down in one avalanche to the level of the vale. The other boy also sank like a stone, and also rose again like a bird, but Smith had no leisure to concern himself with this. For the collapse of that celestial crest had left him standing solitary in the sky on a peak like a church spire.

He could see the tiny figures of the boys in the valley below, and he knew by their attitudes that they were eagerly telling him to jump. Then for the first time he knew the nature of faith, as he had just known the fierce nature of charity. Or rather for the second time, for he remembered one moment when he had known faith before. It was n when his father had taught him to swim, and he had believed he could float on water not only against reason, but (what is so much harder) against instinct. Then he had trusted water; now he must trust air.

He jumped. He went through air and then through snow with the same blinding swiftness. But as he buried himself in solid snow like a bullet he seemed to learn a million things and to learn them all too fast. He knew that the whole world is a snowball, and that all the stars are snowballs. He knew that no man will be fit for heaven till he loves solid whiteness as a little boy loves a ball of snow.

He sank and sank and sank... and then, as usually happens in such cases, woke up, with a start—in the street. True, he was taken up for a common drunk, but (if you properly appreciate his conversion) you will realize that he did not mind; since the crime of drunkenness is infinitely less than that of spiritual pride, of which he had really been guilty.

The High Plains

By high plains I do not mean table-lands; table-lands do not interest one very much. They seem to involve the bore of a climb without the pleasure of a peak. Also they arc vaguely associated with Asia and those enormous armies that eat up everything like locusts, as did the army of Xerxes; with emperors from nowhere spreading their battalions everywhere; with the white elephants and the painted horses, the dark engines and the dreadful mounted bowmen of the moving empires of the East, with all that evil insolence in short that rolled into Europe in the youth of Nero, and after having been battered about and abandoned by one Christian nation after another, turned up in England with Disraeli and was christened (or rather paganed) Imperialism.

Also (it may be necessary to explain) I do not mean "high planes" such as the Theosophists and the Higher Thought Centres talk about. They spell theirs differently; but I will not have theirs in any spelling. They, I know, are always expounding how this or that person is on a lower plane, while they (the speakers) are on a higher plane: sometimes they will almost tell you what plane, as "5994" or "Plane F, sub-plane 304." I do not mean this sort of height either. My religion says nothing about such planes except that all men are on one plane and that by no means a high one. There are saints indeed in my religion: but a saint only means a man who really knows he is a sinner.

Why then should I talk of the plains as high? I do it for a rather singular reason, which I will illustrate by a parallel. When I was at school learning all the Greek I have ever forgotten, I was puzzled by the phrase OINON MELAN that is "black wine," which continually occurred. I asked what it meant, and many most interesting and convincing answers were given. It was pointed out that we know little of the actual liquid drunk by the Greeks; that the analogy of modern Greek wines may suggest that it was dark and sticky, perhaps a sort of syrup always taken with water; that archaic language about colour is always a little dubious, as where Homer speaks of the "wine-dark sea" and so on. I was very properly satisfied, and never thought of the matter again; until one day, having a decanter of claret in front of me, I happened to look at it. I then perceived that they called wine black because it is black. Very thin, diluted, or held-up abruptly against a flame, red wine is red; but seen in body in most normal shades and semi-lights red wine is black, and therefore was called so.

On the same principles I call the plains high because the plains always are high; they are always as high as we are. We talk of climbing a mountain crest and looking down at the plain; but the phrase is an illusion of our arrogance. It is impossible even to look down at the plain. For the plain itself rises as we rise. It is not merely true that the higher we climb the wider and wider is spread out below us the wealth of the world; it is not merely that the devil or some other respectable guide for tourists takes us to the top of an exceeding high mountain and shows us all the kingdoms of the earth. It is more than that, in our real feeling of it. It is that in a sense the whole world rises with us roaring, and accompanies us to the crest like some clanging chorus of eagles. The plains rise higher and higher like swift grey walls piled up against invisible invaders. And however high a peak you climb, the plain is still as high as the peak.

The mountain tops are only noble because from them we are privileged to behold the plains. So the only value in any man being superior is that he may have a superior admiration for the level and the common. If there is any profit in a place craggy and precipitous it is only because from the vale it is not easy to see all the beauty of the vale; because when actually in the flats one cannot see their sublime and satisfying flatness. If there is any value in being educated or eminent (which is doubtful enough) it is only because the best instructed man may feel most swiftly and certainly the splendour of the ignorant and the simple: the full magnificence of that mighty human army in the plains. The general goes up to the hill to look at his soldiers, not to look down at his soldiers. He withdraws himself not because his regiment is too small to be touched, but because it is too mighty to be seen. The chief climbs with submission and goes higher with great humility; since in order to take a bird's eye view of everything, he must become small and distant like a bird.

The most marvellous of those mystical cavaliers who wrote intricate and exquisite verse in England in the seventeenth century, I mean Henry Vaughan, put the matter in one line, intrinsically immortal and practically forgotten—

"Oh holy hope and high humility."

That adjective "high" is not only one of the sudden and stunning inspirations of literature; it is also one of the greatest and gravest definitions of moral science. However far aloft a man may go, he is still looking up, not only at God (which is obvious), but in a manner at men also: seeing more and more all that is towering and mysterious in the dignity and destiny of the lonely house of Adam. I wrote some part of these rambling remarks on a high ridge of rock and turf overlooking a stretch of the central counties; the rise was slight enough in reality, but the immediate ascent had been so steep and sudden that one could not avoid the fancy that on reaching the summit one would look down at the stars. But one did not look down at the stars, but rather up at the cities; seeing as high in heaven the palace town of Alfred like a lit sunset cloud, and away in the void spaces, like a planet in eclipse, Salisbury. So, it may be hoped, until we die you and I will always look up rather than down at the labours and the habitations of our race; we will lift up our eyes to the valleys from whence cometh our help. For from every special eminence and beyond every sublime landmark, it is good for our souls to see only vaster and vaster visions of that dizzy and divine level; and to behold from our crumbling turrets the tall plains of equality.

The Chorus

One of the most marked instances of the decline of true popular sympathy is the gradual disappearance in our time of the habit of singing in chorus. Even when it is done nowadays it is done tentatively and sometimes inaudibly; apparently upon some preposterous principle (which I have never clearly grasped) that singing is an art. In the new aristocracy of the drawing-room a lady is actually asked whether she sings. In the old democracy of the dinner table a man was simply told to sing, and he had to do it. I like the atmosphere of those old banquets. I like to think of my ancestors, middle-aged or venerable gentlemen, all sitting round a table and explaining that they would never forget old days or friends with a rumpty-iddity-iddity, or letting it be known that they would die for England's glory with their tooral ooral, etc. Even the vices of that society (which 'sometimes, I fear, rendered the narrative portions of the song almost as cryptic and inarticulate as the chorus) were displayed with a more human softening than the same vices in the saloon bars of our own time. I greatly prefer Mr. Richard Swiveller to Mr. Stanley Ortheris. I prefer the man who exceeded in rosy wine in order that the wing of friendship might never moult a feather to the man who exceeds quite as much in whiskies and sodas, but declares all the time that he's for number one, and that you don't catch him paying for other men's drinks. The old men of pleasure (with their tooral ooral) got at least some social and communal virtue out of pleasure. The new men of pleasure (without the slightest vestige of a tooral ooral) are simply hermits of irreligion instead of religion, anchorites of atheism, and they might as well be drugging themselves with hashish or opium in a wilderness.

But the chorus of the old songs had another use besides this obvious one of asserting the popular element in the arts. The chorus of a song, even of a comic song, has the same purpose as the chorus in a Greek tragedy. It reconciles men to the gods. It connects this one particular tale with the cosmos and the philosophy of common things, Thus we constantly find in the old ballads, especially the pathetic ballads, some refrain about the grass growing green, or the birds singing, or the woods being merry in spring. These are windows opened in the house of tragedy; momentary glimpses of larger and quieter scenes, of more ancient and enduring landscapes. Many of the country songs describing crime and death have refrains of a startling joviality like cock crow, just as if the whole company were coming in with a shout of protest against so sombre a view of existence. There is a long and gruesome ballad called "The Berkshire Tragedy," about a murder committed by a jealous sister, for the consummation of which a wicked miller is hanged, and the chorus (which should come in a kind of burst) runs:

> *"And I'll be true to my love*
> *If my love'll be true to me."*

G. K. Chesterton

The very reasonable arrangement here suggested is introduced, I think, as a kind of throw back to the normal, a reminder that even "The Berkshire Tragedy" does not fill the whole of Berkshire. The poor young lady is drowned, and the wicked miller (to whom we may have been affectionately attached) is hanged; but still a ruby kindles in the vine, and many a garden by the water blows. Not that Omar's type of hedonistic resignation is at all the same as the breezy impatience of the Berkshire refrain; but they are alike in so far as they gaze out beyond the particular complication to more open plains of peace. The chorus of the ballad looks past the drowning maiden and the miller's gibbet, and sees the lanes full of lovers.

This use of the chorus to humanize and dilute a dark story is strongly opposed to the modern view of art. Modern art has to be what is called "intense." It is not easy to define being intense; but, roughly speaking, it means saying only one thing at a time, and saying it wrong. Modern tragic writers have to write short stories; if they wrote long stories (as the man said of philosophy) cheerfulness would creep in. Such stories are like stings; brief, but purely painful. And doubtless they bore some resemblance to some lives lived under our successful scientific civilization; lives which tend in any case to be painful, and in many cases to be brief. But when the artistic people passed beyond the poignant anecdote and began to write long books full of poignancy, then the reading public began to rebel and to demand the recall of romance. The long books about the black poverty of cities became quite insupportable. The Berkshire tragedy had a chorus; but the London tragedy has no chorus. Therefore people welcomed the return of adventurous novels about alien places and times, the trenchant and swordlike stories of Stevenson. But I am not narrowly on the side of the romantics. I think that glimpses of the gloom of our civilization ought to be recorded. I think that the bewilderments of the solitary and sceptical soul ought to be preserved, if it be only for the pity (yes, and the admiration) of a happier time. But I wish that there were some way in which the chorus could enter. I wish that at the end of each chapter of stiff agony or insane terror the choir of humanity could come in with a crash of music and tell both the reader and the author that this is not the whole of human experience. Let them go on recording hard scenes or hideous questions, but let there be a jolly refrain.

Thus we might read: "As Honoria laid down the volume of Ibsen and went wearily to her window, she realized that life must be to her not only harsher, but colder than it was to the comfortable and the weak. With her tooral ooral, etc.;" or, again: "The young curate smiled grimly as he listened to his great-grandmother's last words. He knew only too well that since Phogg's discovery of the hereditary hairiness of goats religion stood on a very different basis from that which it had occupied in his childhood. With his rumpty-iddity, rumpty-iddity;" and so on. Or we might read: "Uriel Maybloom stared gloomily down at his sandals, as he realized for the first time how senseless and anti-social are all ties between man and woman; how each must go his or her way without any attempt to arrest the head-long separation of their souls." And then would come in one deafening chorus of everlasting humanity "But I'll be true to my love, if my love'll be true to me."

In the records of the first majestic and yet fantastic developments of the foundation of St. Francis of Assisi is an account of a certain Blessed Brother Giles. I have forgotten most of it, but I remember one fact: that certain students of theology came to ask him whether he believed in free will, and, if so, how he could reconcile it with necessity. On hearing the question St. Francis's follower reflected a little while and then seized a fiddle and began capering and dancing about the garden, playing a wild tune and generally expressing a violent and invigorating indifference. The tune is not recorded, but it is the eternal chorus of mankind, that modifies all the arts and mocks all the individualisms, like the laughter and thunder of some distant sea.

G. K. Chesterton

A Romance of the Marshes

In books as a whole marshes are described as desolate and colourless, great fields of clay or sedge, vast horizons of drab or grey. But this, like many other literary associations, is a piece of poetical injustice. Monotony has nothing to do with a place; monotony, either in its sensation or its infliction, is simply the quality of a person. There are no dreary sights; there are only dreary sightseers. It is a matter of taste, that is of personality, whether marshes are monotonous; but it is a matter of fact and science that they are not monochrome. The tops of high mountains (I am told) are all white; the depths of primeval caverns (I am also told) are all dark. The sea will be grey or blue for weeks together; and the desert, I have been led to believe, is the colour of sand. The North Pole (if we found it) would be white with cracks of blue; and Endless Space (if we went there) would, I suppose, be black with white spots. If any of these were counted of a monotonous colour I could well understand it; but on the contrary, they are always spoken of as if they had the gorgeous and chaotic colours of a cosmic kaleidoscope. Now exactly where you can find colours like those of a tulip garden or a stained-glass window, is in those sunken and sodden lands which are always called dreary. Of course the great tulip gardens did arise in Holland; which is simply one immense marsh. There is nothing in Europe so truly tropical as marshes. Also, now I come to think of it, there are few places so agreeably marshy as tropics. At any rate swamp and fenlands in England are always especially rich in gay grasses or gorgeous fungoids; and seem sometimes as glorious as a transformation scene; but also as unsubstantial. In these splendid scenes it is always very easy to put your foot through the scenery. You may sink up to your armpits; but you will sink up to your armpits in flowers. I do not deny that I myself am of a sort that sinks—except in the matter of spirits. I saw in the west counties recently a swampy field of great richness and promise. If I had stepped on it I have no doubt at all that I should have vanished; that aeons hence the complete fossil of a fat Fleet Street journalist would be found in that compressed clay. I only claim that it would be found in some attitude of energy, or even of joy. But the last point is the most important of all, for as I imagined myself sinking up to the neck in what looked like a solid green field, I suddenly remembered that this very thing must have happened to certain interesting pirates quite a thousand years ago.

For, as it happened, the flat fenland in which I so nearly sunk was the fenland round the Island of Athelney, which is now an island in the fields and no longer in the waters. But on the abrupt hillock a stone still stands to say that this was that embattled islet in the Parrett where King Alfred held his last fort against the foreign invaders, in that war that nearly washed us as far from civilization as the Solomon Islands. Here he defended the island called Athelney as he afterwards did his best to defend the island called England. For the hero always defends an island, a thing beleaguered

Alarms and Discursions

and surrounded, like the Troy of Hector. And the highest and largest humanitarian can only rise to defending the tiny island called the earth.

One approaches the island of Athelney along a low long road like an interminable white string stretched across the flats, and lined with those dwarfish trees that are elvish in their very dullness. At one point of the journey (I cannot conceive why) one is arrested by a toll gate at which one has to pay threepence. Perhaps it is a distorted tradition of those dark ages. Perhaps Alfred, with the superior science of comparative civilization, had calculated the economics of Denmark down to a halfpenny. Perhaps a Dane sometimes came with twopence, sometimes even with twopence-halfpenny, after the sack of many cities even with twopence three farthings; but never with threepence. Whether or no it was a permanent barrier to the barbarians it was only a temporary barrier to me. I discovered three large and complete coppers in various parts of my person, and I passed on along that strangely monotonous and strangely fascinating path. It is not merely fanciful to feel that the place expresses itself appropriately as the place where the great Christian King hid himself from the heathen. Though a marshland is always open it is still curiously secret. Fens, like deserts, are large things very apt to be mislaid. These flats feared to be overlooked in a double sense; the small trees crouched and the whole plain seemed lying on its face, as men do when shells burst. The little path ran fearlessly forward; but it seemed to run on all fours. Everything in that strange countryside seemed to be lying low, as if to avoid the incessant and rattling rain of the Danish arrows. There were indeed hills of no inconsiderable height quite within call; but those pools and flats of the old Parrett seemed to separate themselves like a central and secret sea; and in the midst of them stood up the rock of Athelney as isolate as it was to Alfred. And all across this recumbent and almost crawling country there ran the glory of the low wet lands; grass lustrous and living like the plumage of some universal bird; the flowers as gorgeous as bonfires and the weeds more beautiful than the flowers. One stooped to stroke the grass, as if the earth were all one kind beast that could feel.

Why does no decent person write an historical novel about Alfred and his fort in Athelney, in the marshes of the Parrett? Not a very historical novel. Not about his Truth-telling (please) or his founding the British Empire, or the British Navy, or the Navy League, or whichever it was he founded. Not about the Treaty of Wedmore and whether it ought (as an eminent historian says) to be called the Pact of Chippenham. But an aboriginal romance for boys about the bare, bald, beatific fact that a great hero held his fort in an island in a river. An island is fine enough, in all conscience or piratic unconscientiousness, but an island in a river sounds like the beginning of the greatest adventure story on earth. "Robinson Crusoe" is really a great tale, but think of Robinson Crusoe's feelings if he could have actually seen England and Spain from his inaccessible isle! "Treasure Island" is a spirit of genius: but what treasure could an island contain to compare with Alfred? And then consider the further elements of juvenile romance in an island that was more of an island than it looked.

G. K. Chesterton

Athelney was masked with marshes; many a heavy harnessed Viking may have started bounding across a meadow only to find himself submerged in a sea. I feel the full fictitious splendour spreading round me; I see glimpses of a great romance that will never be written. I see a sudden shaft quivering in one of the short trees. I see a red-haired man wading madly among the tall gold flowers of the marsh, leaping onward and lurching lower. I see another shaft stand quivering in his throat. I cannot see any more, because, as I have delicately suggested, I am a heavy man. This mysterious marshland does not sustain me, and I sink into its depths with a bubbling groan.

The Meaning of Life and Other Useless Crap is perhaps our generations greatest work as it answers the age old question "What is the meaning of life?" Written simply and straightforward it is easy to understand why Ben Lemon is the most important living philosopher. It hasn't been since A Modest Proposal that a pamphlet can our perceptions so dramatically.

Made in the USA
Monee, IL
11 April 2022